Sunderland Football Club
An A-Z

SUNDERLAND FOOTBALL CLUB AN A-Z

Dean Hayes

Aureus

First Published 1999

©1999 Dean Hayes

Printed in Great Britain.

A catalogue record for this book is available from the British Library.

Aureus Publishing 24 Mafeking Road Cardiff CF23 5DQ.

ISBN 1 899750 14 2

A

ABANDONED MATCHES

A match which is called off by the referee whilst it is in progress, because conditions do not permit it to be completed. Generally speaking, far fewer matches are now abandoned because if there is some doubt about the ability to play the full game, the match is more likely to be postponed.

One match which was 'abandoned' just before kick-off was the Newcastle United v Sunderland game on Good Friday 1901. Fighting broke out among the 50,000 crowd and corner flags and goal posts were torn down. The playing surface was turned into a ploughed field and the referee had no alternative but to 'abandon' the game. In the rearranged fixture at the end of the season, Sunderland won 2-0.

Drawn against First Division Manchester City in the second round of the 1912-13 FA Cup competition, Sunderland built up a 2-0 lead early in the second half. The large and enthusiastic crowd at the old Hyde Road ground however, had started to encroach onto the pitch, leaving the referee with little option but to abandon the game with 25 minutes to go. An FA inquiry ruled that the game should be played at Roker Park and the Wearsiders went through at the second attempt 2-0.

The last game to be abandoned involving Sunderland was their home match against Liverpool on 12 January 1985 with the game goalless. When the game was replayed the following April, the Merseyside outfit won 3-0.

ADAMSON, JIMMY

Ashington-born Jimmy Adamson began his league career with Burnley, but his early years at Turf Moor were something of a struggle. Adamson was still playing as an inside-forward and it was only after his conversion to wing-half that his true potential started to be realised.

Adamson replaced Reg Attwell for the match at Bolton Wanderers in February 1951 which the Clarets drew 1-1 and over the next 13 seasons he was a virtual ever-present in the Burnley side. In March 1953 he was chosen to represent England 'B' in the first-ever meeting with Scotland 'B' in Edinburgh. When the club won the League Championship in 1959-60, Adamson played in every match and in October 1960, the popular Burnley player received another belated honour when he was selected to represent the Football League against the Irish League at Bloomfield Road.

In 1961-62 the Clarets came close to doing the League and Cup double but were pipped at the post by Ipswich in the League and then lost to Spurs in the FA Cup Final at Wembley. In recognition of the club's magnificent achievement, Adamson the Burnley captain was voted Footballer of the Year. In 1962 he was chosen as a member of the England squad for the World Cup Finals in Chile and on the resignation of Walter Winterbottom was offered the England manager's job. He felt he couldn't accept the position because of his lack of managerial experience.

Jimmy Adamson who played in 486 first team games for the Clarets eventually succeeded Harry Potts as Burnley manager and though the club lost their First Division status in 1970-71, he led the Lancashire club to the Second Division Championship in 1972-73. He left Turf Moor in January 1976 and after a brief spell with Sparta Rotterdam he became manager of Sunderland, replacing FA Cup hero, Bob Stokoe.

Unfortunately, he was unable to prevent the Wearsiders' relegation to the Second Division at the end of his first season with the club. In 1977-78 the club looked as though they would return to the top flight at the first attempt but results towards the end of the campaign went against them and they finished sixth. Adamson who had something of a love-hate relationship with Sunderland supporters left the club in October 1978 to take over from Jock Stein as manager of Leeds United.

He took the Elland Road club into Europe and to a League Cup semi-final but after a poor start to the 1980-81 season, he resigned and left the game for good.

Sunderland's full league record under Jimmy Adamson is:

P	W	D	L	F	A
79	28	26	25	116	104

AGGREGATE SCORE

Sunderland's highest aggregate score in any competition came in the Football League Cup of 1990-91. Playing Bristol City, the Wearsiders lost 1-0 at home before winning the second leg at Ashton Gate 6-1. The club's scorers on that memorable night in Bristol were Gabbiadini (2), Ball, Owers, Hauser and Cullen.

AITKEN, GEORGE

Wing-half George Aitken began his career with East Fife where he won the first of his eight full caps for Scotland. Playing against England at Wembley, Aitken starred in a 3-1 win for the Scots. He later played for Third Lanark, from where he joined Sunderland in November 1951 for a fee of £20,000.

His first game in the red and white stripes of the Wearsiders was in a 2-2 draw at home to Fulham, though in his first season at Roker Park he shared the number six shirt with Arthur Wright. For the next six seasons, Aitken was a virtual ever-present in the Sunderland side and though he only scored three goals for the club, the Wearsiders never lost when he was on the scoresheet.

The Lochgelly-born player went on to appear in 267 League and Cup games for Sunderland before leaving the club in May 1959 to play for Gateshead where he made 58 league appearances.

ANDERSON, STAN

Stan Anderson had the distinction of captaining all three major north-east clubs, Sunderland, Newcastle United and Middlesbrough.

He made his Football League debut for Sunderland in a 1-1 draw at home to Portsmouth on 9 October 1952 and over the next 11 seasons was a virtual ever-present in the Wearsiders' team. The tough-tackling wing-half was capped twice for England, playing against Austria and Scotland in 1962, but on the domestic front, failed to win any honours, though he did appear in two FA Cup semi-finals for Sunderland. He had scored 35 goals in 447 League and Cup games for the Wearsiders when in November 1963 he joined Newcastle United for a fee of £19,000.

His move to St James' Park shocked the Sunderland faithful who were soon to see their club promoted to the First Division. Anderson made a dramatic impact on the Newcastle side and was instrumental in their promotion from the Second Division in 1964-65. He never added to his collection of full caps, the reason for this probably being due to the fact that he was sent-off in an Under-23 international against Bulgaria in 1957.

After joining Middlesbrough, first as player-coach, he was appointed manager in April 1966 and brought about a revival at Ayresome Park. Unfortunately his appointment came too late to save the Teeside club from relegation but in 1966-67 he led them back to the Second Division. After twice going close to promotion to the First Division, he left to manage AEK Athens.

After short spells with Queen's Park Rangers, Manchester City and Doncaster Rovers, he joined Bolton Wanderers as coach under manager Ian Greaves. When Greaves was dismissed in January 1980, Anderson took over as caretaker-manager before the appointment was made official the following month. At the end of that season, the Wanderers were relegated and in March 1981 with results still not improving, another former Sunderland favourite, George Mulhall returned to the club as Anderson's assistant. It was his return that coincided with the club's run to safety and in May 1981, Stan Anderson was sacked with almost two years of his contract still to run.

Stan Anderson

ANDREWS, ARTHUR

Signed from Durham City in November 1922, wing-half Arthur Andrews played his first game in Sunderland colours on 9 December 1922 in a 1-1 draw at Everton. After making just one more appearance that campaign, he became an established member of the Sunderland side in 1923-24 and was a virtual ever-present for the next eight seasons. Andrews played all of his football for Sunderland in the First Division and helped the Wearsiders to finish third in the top flight on three occasions.

Though he only scored two goals during his Sunderland career, they were both spectacular efforts and came in the 4-1 win at Aston Villa on 4 April 1925 and in a 5-1 home defeat of Sheffield Wednesday on 7 March 1931 after which he played in just two more games for the club.

He had played in 244 first team games for Sunderland when at the end of March 1931 he moved into non-League football with Blyth Spartans.

ANGLO-ITALIAN CUP

When Swindon Town won the Football League Cup in 1969, they were ineligible for the Fairs Cup because they were not a First Division side. Consequently, they organised a match against the Italian League Cup winners, AS Roma, playing for the Anglo-Italian League Cup. The following year the Anglo-Italian Cup was introduced for club sides from the two countries who had no involvement in Europe.

Sunderland first entered at the end of the 1969-70 season. Their results were:

| Lazio | (Home) 3-1 | (Away) 1-2 |
| Fiorentina | (Home) 2-2 | (Away) 0-3 |

They next entered in 1971-72 when their results were:

| Atalanta | (Home) 0-0 | (Away) 2-3 |
| Cagliari | (Home) 3-3 | (Away) 3-1 |

Sunderland next entered the competition when it was reintroduced in 1992-93. Their results in the group matches against Cambridge United (Away 1-1) and Birmingham City (Home 0-1) failed to qualify them for matches against their Italian counterparts as it did in 1993-94 when they played Tranmere Rovers (Home 2-0) and Bolton Wanderers (Away 0-2).

ANGLO-SCOTTISH CUP

The Anglo-Scottish Cup was inaugurated in 1975-76 following the withdrawal of Texaco from the competition of that name. The first winners were Middlesbrough who beat Fulham 1-0 on aggregate.

Sunderland only entered the competition in the 1978-79 season but failed to qualify for the knockout stages after the following group results - Bolton Wanderers (Home 2-0) Oldham Athletic (Away 1-2) and Burnley (Away 1-2).

APPEARANCES

Jim Montgomery holds the club record for the number of League and Cup appearances with a total of 623 games to his credit in 16 seasons with the Wearsiders.

The players with the highest number of appearances are as follows:

		League	FA Cup	FLg Cup	Others	Total
1	Jim Montgomery	537	41	33	12	623
2	Ned Doig	421	35	-	-	456
3	Len Ashurst	403(12)	26(2)	23	-	452(14)
4	Stan Anderson	402	34	11	-	447
5	Gary Bennett	368(10)	17(2)	34(1)	16	435(13)
6	Bobby Kerr	355(22)	29(1)	14	15	413(23)
7	Charlie Buchan	380	33	-	-	413
8	Charlie Hurley	357(2)	26	17	-	400(2)
9	Gordon Armstrong	331(18)	19	25(4)	18(1)	393(23)
10	Bob Gurney	348	40	-	-	388

ARMSTRONG, GORDON

Though he was born on Tyneside, Gordon Armstrong has always been a red and white fanatic from the day he joined the club as an apprentice from St Montague Juniors, Newcastle.

After working his way through the ranks, he made his first team debut in a 1-0 defeat at West Bromwich Albion on 24 April 1985, at the end of a season in which the club were relegated to the Second Division. After establishing himself in the Sunderland side midway through the following season, he missed very few games over the next nine campaigns and was ever-present in seasons 1986-87 and 1989-90. He won a Third Division Championship medal in 1987-88 and was an important member of the side that won promotion to the First Division in 1989-90 after Swindon Town had lost their place in the top flight following investigations by the Inland Revenue and the Football League.

Armstrong's best season in terms of goals scored was 1991-92 when he found the net 10 times in 41 league games, though none of his strikes that term was as important as his brilliant last minute header against Chelsea that took the Wearsiders into the FA Cup semi-final against Norwich City. Awarded a testimonial for his loyal service to the club in 1993-94, 'Stretch' scored 61 goals in 418 first team games. Following loan spells with Bristol City and Northampton Town he joined Bury on a free transfer in July 1996.

Though he missed the early part of the Shakers' 1996-97 campaign through a recurring hamstring injury, he figured in the side at left-back from March onwards and won a Second Division Championship medal. The following season he switched to a sweeper's role and was a revelation as the Gigg Lane club sought to consolidate in a higher league.

ARNOTT, KEVIN

Gateshead-born midfielder Kevin Arnott first appeared in the Sunderland side midway through the club's relegation season of 1976-77, in a 2-0 defeat at Leicester City, after which he played in every one of the 20 games that remained of that campaign. After two seasons in and out of

Kevin Arnott

7

the Sunderland side, he won a regular first team place in 1979-80 as the club finished runners-up in the Second Division to Leicester City. That season was his best in terms of goals scored, as he netted eight in games which the club either won or drew, including one in the final game of the campaign against West Ham United.

After an impressive first season in the top flight, he lost his place and went on loan to Blackburn Rovers before signing for Sheffield United in May 1982. Arnott who had scored 17 goals in 153 games, gave the Blades five seasons good service, but following loan spells at Blackburn a second time and Rotherham United, he left to play for Swedish club Vasalund. Arnott later returned to this country to see out his career with Chesterfield.

ASHURST, JACKIE
Jackie Ashurst joined Sunderland as an apprentice in 1969 and turned professional in October 1971. He made his debut for the Wearsiders in a 3-2 Anglo-Italian Cup defeat in Atalanta in June 1972 before making his league debut in a 1-0 win at Millwall in September of that year.

Jackie Ashurst

He was in the Sunderland squad for the 1973 FA Cup Final, although injury ruled him out of the Wembley game. He won a Division Two Championship medal in 1975-76 and would have made many more than the 178 appearances he did make had it not been for the presence of Dave Watson at centre-half.

In October 1979, Ashurst left Roker Park to join Blackpool for £110,000 where he was used mainly as a utility player. Sadly injuries then curtailed his appearances and in August 1981 he was allowed to join Carlisle United for £40,000. Then in the summer of 1986 he was transferred to Leeds United where he skippered the side in the absence of Snodin and Aizlewood. His next port of call was Doncaster Rovers in October 1988. Released in the summer of 1990, he spent a short time with Bridlington Town before rejoining Doncaster in November 1990. He played one game for Rochdale before ending his career with North Shields.

ASHURST, LEN

Liverpool-born Len Ashurst began his career with local non-League club Prescot Cables before joining Sunderland in December 1957. A steady and constructive full-back, he made his first team debut on 20 September 1958 in a 2-0 home defeat by Ipswich Town.

He soon established himself as a first team regular and over the next 12 seasons, hardly missed a match. He was ever-present in 1961-62 and again in 1963-64 when the club won promotion to the First Division as runners-up to Leeds United. That season, Ashurst, who only scored four goals in 466 League and Cup appearances for the Wearsiders, scored the winner in a 2-1 defeat of Newcastle United, watched by a Roker Park crowd of 56,903.

After playing his last game for the club at Coventry City in March 1970, Ashurst moved to Hartlepool United as player-manager.

In the summer of 1974 he became manager of Gillingham before joining Sheffield Wednesday in October 1975. Though he was unable to get the Owls out of the Third Division, he did make a number of important signings which were of long-term benefit to the Hillsborough club.

He later managed Newport County, leading the Ironsides to promotion, the Welsh Cup and entry into Europe before moving to Cardiff City and helping the Ninian Park club to promotion from the Third Division.

In March 1984 he returned to Roker Park as Sunderland manager but had a very unhappy spell at his former club as they lost to Norwich City in the League Cup Final and were relegated to the Second Division. He was sacked soon afterwards.

He then went abroad to coach in Kuwait and Qatar before returning to these shores to become assistant-manager at Blackpool before taking full charge at Cardiff City a second time. However, the Bluebirds were relegated to the Fourth Division in 1990 and after another poor season, he was sacked.

Sunderland's full league record under Len Ashurst is:

P	W	D	L	F	A
55	15	13	27	52	74

Len Ashurst

ATTENDANCES - AVERAGE

The average home league attendances of Sunderland over the last ten seasons have been as follows:

1988-89	14,878	1993-94	16,934
1989-90	17,728	1994-95	15,344
1990-91	22,577	1995-96	17,482
1991-92	18,390	1996-97	20,865
1992-93	17,258	1997-98	33,492

ATTENDANCE - HIGHEST

The club's record attendance is 75,118 for the sixth round FA Cup replay against Derby County on 8 March 1933. The match ended in a 1-0 win for the Rams after the first game at the Baseball Ground had ended 4-4. The record attendance for a league match is 68,004, on 4 March 1950 when Sunderland drew 2-2 with rivals Newcastle United. Ivor Broadis and Len Shackleton scored the club's goals.

ATTENDANCE - LOWEST

The lowest attendance at Roker Park is probably the 3,911 for the visit of Portsmouth in a First Division game on 29 April 1933. For the record, the Fratton Park club won 3-0.

AWAY MATCHES

Sunderland's best away win is the 9-1 victory over Newcastle United on 5 December 1908. The club have also scored seven goals away from home on two occasions, winning 7-1 at Darwen in April 1892 and 7-2 at Birmingham during the Championship-winning season of 1935-36.

Sunderland's worst defeat away from home is 8-0, a scoreline inflicted upon them by three clubs - Sheffield Wednesday (1911-12) West Ham United (1968-69) and Watford (1982-83).

Sunderland have also been involved in two high scoring matches away from home, losing 6-5 on both occasions to West Bromwich Albion in 1933-34 and to Derby County in 1950-51.

AWAY SEASONS

The club's highest number of away wins came in 1987-88 when they won 13 of their 23 matches in winning the Third Division Championship. The club's lowest number of away wins - one, occurred in 1965-66 and 1968-69.

B

BALL, KEVIN

Sunderland midfielder and captain Kevin Ball began his Football League career with Portsmouth whom he joined on a free transfer from Coventry City juniors in October 1982. The Hastings-born player made his debut for Pompey in January 1984 in a 2-0 defeat at Shrewsbury Town, going on to appear in 128 first team games before his £350,000 transfer to the Wearsiders in the summer of 1990.

He made his debut for Sunderland in a goalless home draw against Tottenham Hotspur on 28 August 1990 and since then has been a virtual ever-present in the side. It was after he moved from his usual central defensive position that he formed an outstanding midfield partnership with Paul Bracewell. During the 1995-96 First Division championship-winning season, he scored four vital goals including a late winner against Oldham Athletic.

During the club's stint in the Premiership, Ball continued to produce a string of whole-hearted displays and ended the 1996-97 campaign as the club's joint-top scorer with four goals! In 1997-98 he continued to score a number of important goals including a superb left-foot volley in the play-off semi-final at Sheffield United.

Captaining the club to the First Division Championship in 1998-99, Kevin Ball is very popular on Wearside because of his total commitment and will to win. The inspirational captain who is now in his ninth season with Sunderland has scored 24 goals in 329 games.

BAXTER, JIM

Born in the Fife village of Hill O'Beath, he served a brief apprenticeship as a cabinet maker in nearby Dunfermline before going down the pit. After beginning his career with Crossgates Primrose, he joined Raith Rovers in the summer of 1957. Baxter was earning rave reviews and it became obvious that Raith Rovers would be unable to hold on to such precocious talent for long.

In the summer of 1960 and with a number of clubs expressing an interest, Rangers' manager Scot Symon paid £27,000 to secure Baxter's services.

His liking for alcohol was becoming almost as legendary as his skills on the football field, yet despite this, he was still able to control the play in the middle of the park.

He won the first of his 34 caps for Scotland against Northern Ireland in 1961 and in 1963 scored both his country's goals in a 2-1 win over England at Wembley. In 1967 he was to perform similar heroics, inspiring Scotland to a 3-2 victory over the reigning World Champions. He was probably at his peak in 1963 when he was chosen for the Rest of the World in the match to celebrate the centenary of the Football Association.

In the close season of 1965, Baxter left Ibrox Park, signing for Sunderland for £80,000, a move which surprised most football observers. After making his debut in a 1-0 defeat at Leeds United on the opening day of the 1965-66 season, he quickly became a big fish in a small pond, despite Sunderland's status in the game. At the end of his first season at Roker Park, the Wearsiders finished just three points off the drop and Baxter found it a frustrating experience. After two-and-a-half unhappy seasons at Sunderland in which he scored 12 goals in 98 games, he signed for Nottingham Forest for £100,000.

His spell at the City Ground lasted less than two years and after being given a free transfer, he rejoined Rangers. But the years of drinking and gambling had taken their toll and after just one season he was given his second free transfer and a glittering career was at an end.

BENNETT, GARY

Manchester-born Gary Bennett, brother of Dave, began his career with Ashton United before joining Manchester City in September 1979. Unable to break into the Maine Road club's first team, he joined Cardiff City on a free transfer two years later.

He made his League debut for the Bluebirds in a 3-2 home win over Wrexham, two months after arriving at Ninian Park but it was 1982-83 before he established himself as a first team regular. Though he played both in midfield and in attack for the Welsh side, his best position was in the centre of defence. He had scored 12 goals in 96 first team games when he was transferred to Sunderland for £65,000 in July 1984.

He made his debut for the Wearsiders in a 3-1 home win over Southampton on the opening day of the 1984-85 season and scored against England 'keeper Peter Shilton within two minutes! The following season he was at centre-half in the League Cup Final defeat by Norwich City and in 1987-88 when the club won the Third Division Championship, he was the only member of the Sunderland side to be selected for the annual PFA XI.

A virtual ever-present in eleven seasons at Roker Park, he scored 24 goals in 463 League and Cup appearances before he joined Carlisle United on a free transfer in November 1995.

The powerful defender was hampered by injuries during his stay at Brunton Park and at the end of the 1995-96 season, he joined Scarborough.

In 1996-97 he played in every match and was voted the North East Player of the Year by the Sunday Sun, an award he won for a second successive year after enjoying a wonderful season with the Yorkshire club.

BEST STARTS

Sunderland were unbeaten for the first 18 games of the 1998-99 First Division season when they won 11 and drew seven of their matches. Their first defeat came at home to Barnsley on 21 November 1998 when they went down 3-2.

BINGHAM, BILLY

Billy Bingham started his illustrious career with Irish League Glentoran, though it was Sunderland who introduced him to English football in 1950. He played his first game for the Wearsiders in a 1-1 home draw against Stoke City on 2 December 1950.

Within two years of his arrival at Roker Park, he was a permanent member of the Northern Ireland team. All told, he won 56 caps equalling Danny Blanchflower's record until the record was surpassed by Terry Neill.

Bingham was a superb dribbler and crosser of the ball, loving nothing better than to face an opponent in a one-to-one situation. The highlight of his international career was helping the Irishmen get all the way to the World Cup quarter-finals in Sweden in 1958.

He scored 47 goals in 227 games for Sunderland before joining Luton

Town for £15,000 during the summer of 1958. He arrived at Goodison Park in October 1960 and won a League Championship medal in 1962-63 before leaving for Port Vale, where a broken leg brought an end to his playing days.

He became manager of Southport, leading them to promotion for the first time in their history. After spells at Plymouth and Linfield, he took charge of the Greek national side before returning to Everton as manager in May 1973. He inherited a team badly in need of major reconstruction but took the team to seventh in the First Division, a huge improvement on the previous two seasons.

In 1974-75 the club came fourth but in January 1977 with the Blues in 13th place, he was sacked.

He later took charge at Mansfield Town and led the Northern Ireland team to the World Cup Finals in 1982 and 1986.

BOLTON, JOE
Tough-tackling left-back Joe Bolton gave the club great service appearing in 324 League and Cup games during 10 seasons at Roker Park. After working his way through the ranks, he made his first team debut in a 5-0 home win over Watford on 17 April 1972. Never afraid to shoot from distance, the first of his 12 goals for the club came in a 4-0 defeat of Brighton and Hove Albion at Roker Park in January 1973.

Joe Bolton

15

After helping the club win the Second Division Championship in 1975-76, Bolton was the only ever-present in Sunderland's return to the top flight but it lasted just one season as they made a hasty return to Division Two.

The long-serving Bolton was also a key member of Ken Knighton's promotion-winning side in 1979-80 but after appearing in most of the club's First Division games the following season, he left to join Middlesbrough for a fee of £200,000.

In two seasons at Ayresome Park, he appeared in 59 league games before leaving to end his league career with Sheffield United in the summer of 1983. He played in 109 league games for the Bramall Lane club before leaving the scene to work as a lorry driver for a Sheffield haulage firm.

BRACEWELL, PAUL

Paul Bracewell battled through the ranks at Stoke City to make his first team debut before his 18th birthday. With three full seasons and 141 appearances behind him, he followed Alan Durban to Sunderland for £250,000 in June 1983.

He made his debut for the Wearsiders in a 1-1 home draw against Norwich City on the opening day of the 1983-84 season but at the end of a fairly unsuccessful campaign, he left the club to join Everton.

He holds the rare distinction of making his Everton debut at Wembley as he played in the Charity Shield showpiece against Liverpool in August 1984. Forming a good understanding with Peter Reid in the Everton midfield, he won his first England cap when he replaced Bryan Robson against West Germany on the summer tour to Mexico. On New Year's Day 1986, Bracewell suffered a serious ankle injury in a 2-2 draw at Newcastle United and was out of the game for 20 months. During this time he had undergone five operations and towards the end of the 1987-88 campaign, he was forced to undergo even more surgery on his right ankle. He had appeared in 135 first team games, winning League Championship and European Cup Winners' Cup medals when in September 1989 he rejoined Sunderland in a £250,000 transfer following a loan spell.

He helped the club win promotion to the top flight in 1989-90 and played for the Wearsiders in the 1992 FA Cup Final - the fourth time he had picked up a runners-up medal - before joining Newcastle United.

He made a telling contribution to the Magpies' promotion to the Premier League before in the summer of 1995 he returned to Sunderland for his third spell with the club.

As player/assistant-manager, Bracewell's experience proved vital as

Sunderland went back to the top flight as First Division champions. In 1996-97, Bracewell was the club's only ever-present in the Premier League but after just three games of the following campaign, he became Kevin Keegan's first signing when he joined Fulham for £75,000. Bracewell, who had appeared in 270 games for Sunderland was voted into the PFA award-winning Second Division side after just one season at Craven Cottage, where he is now the manager.

BRIDGETT, ARTHUR

A fleet-footed left-winger, Arthur Bridgett played for Burslem Park Boys and Trentham before beginning his league career with Stoke. He joined Sunderland in January 1903 and made his debut in a goalless draw at home to Sheffield United midway through that month. Bridgett was the club's first choice outside-left for ten seasons, winning the first of 11 England caps against Scotland in 1905. He scored three goals for England including one in each game against Austria in the space of three days in June 1908 which England won 6-1 and 11-1. In fact, Bridgett never played on a losing side when turning out for his country.

In 1906-07, Bridgett established a new club record, later equalled by Dave Halliday and Raich Carter of scoring in eight consecutive league games. In May 1912 after netting 119 goals in 347 League and Cup games, he left Roker Park to join South Shields as manager. He later held a similar post with North Shields but during the war he joined Port Vale. He rejoined the Burslem club in November 1923 at the age of 41 and scored inside the first minute of his comeback game against Clapton Orient. He later left Vale Park and ended his career with Sandbach Ramblers.

BROADIS, IVOR

Ivor Broadis was one of the most skilful inside-forwards of his generation, a player with excellent ball control, the ability to make space and create chances for others and a keen eye for goal that brought him his fair share of goals.

Though he started his playing career at White Hart Lane, playing for Tottenham juniors and later Finchley and Northfleet, it was with Manchester City and Newcastle United that he enjoyed his best days. After making his Spurs debut against Clapton Orient in the London War Cup in January 1941, he played regularly for the next 18 months. However, after joining the armed forces he wasn't so readily available for Spurs and 'guested' for Bradford Park Avenue, Manchester United and Millwall.

In August 1946, Carlisle United offered him professional terms, not only as a player but as player-manager. He was highly successful with the Third Division (North) club and in February 1949 transferred himself to Sunderland for £18,000.

He played his first game for the Wearsiders in a 5-0 defeat at Arsenal and ended the campaign with just two goals in 13 appearances. In 1949-50 he was back to top form, missing just one game, and he scored 13 goals as Sunderland finished third in Division One. His form led to him being a member of England's 1950 World Cup squad. On Boxing Day 1950 he netted his only hat-trick for the club in a 5-3 win against Manchester United at Old Trafford. He had scored 27 goals in 84 games when in October 1951 he joined Manchester City for £20,000. A month later he made his England debut against Austria and won another seven caps before moving to Newcastle United in October 1953. At St James' Park he won another six caps and an FA Cup winners' medal in 1955.

At the end of that season, he moved back to Carlisle United as player-coach and played for them for another three years before finishing his playing career with one year at Queen of the South.

BROWN, ALAN

Alan Brown made his name as a manager through his ability to discover good young players and develop them.

He signed for Huddersfield Town in 1933, though in the five seasons leading up to the Second World War he never really established himself as a first team regular and only made 38 league appearances. During the war he 'guested' for Liverpool, Manchester United and Notts County and in 1945 he was selected as a reserve for the England team to play Scotland at Villa Park.

In February 1946 he joined Burnley and was immediately appointed captain. In his first season with the club, Brown was ever-present and led the Clarets to promotion from the Second Division and to Wembley as FA Cup runners-up to Charlton Athletic.

He won his only representative honour when he captained the Football League to a 4-3 win over the Irish League in Belfast in 1948. He later played for Notts County before joining Sheffield Wednesday as a coach in 1951. In 1954 he returned to Turf Moor as manager and had three moderately successful years before becoming Sunderland's manager in the summer of 1957.

Unfortunately, his first season at Roker Park saw the club relegated from the top flight, the club's first since joining the Football League in 1890! He unearthed a number of future stars, including the great Charlie Hurley, who was signed from Millwall. In 1963-64 he led the Wearsiders back to the top flight but rather than enjoy his new success, he moved to Sheffield Wednesday as manager. He took the Owls to the FA Cup Final of 1966 but two years later he was back at Roker Park.

His return to the club was marred when the Wearsiders were relegated to the Second Division in 1969-70. The Sunderland manager was criticised for supposedly being more interested in developing young players than dealing with the more complex problems of the club's established professionals. The club challenged for promotion in 1971-72 but midway through the following season, he was sacked.

He later coached in Norway and, after returning to England, assisted Plymouth Argyle before retiring.

Sunderland's full league record under Alan Brown is:

P	W	D	L	F	A
476	175	136	165	704	706

BUCHAN, CHARLIE

Charlie Buchan was one of four brothers - three of whom became professional footballers - the son of an Aberdonian colour-sergeant who became a blacksmith in the Woolwich Arsenal: hence Buchan's South East London birth and background.

In November 1909, Buchan a 17-year-old still attending the Woolwich Polytechnic and playing for Woolwich Arsenal reserves, put in an expense account for 11 shillings (55 pence). George Morrell the club manager, high-handedly refused to pay it. Buchan left and after a spell with the amateurs Northfleet, turned professional with Leyton in the Southern League. In March 1911 following a splendid game against Southampton, he joined Sunderland.

He made his debut for the Wearsiders in a 1-1 draw at Tottenham Hotspur on 1 April 1911. The Sunderland team in which he played before the First World War was indeed a 'team of all the talents', Buchan forming a splendid triangle with winger Jackie Mordue and right-half Frank Cuggy and a fine partnership with that other powerful inside-forward whom he so much admired, George Holley.

Buchan, a true Londoner, did not even know where Sunderland was when they signed him! His success in the team was not immediate. For one thing, he was still growing fast and after each training session he was too weak to do anything but lie on his couch in a vacant and pensive mood. The Roker Park crowd began to get at him and he asked to be dropped but manager Bob Kyle stoutly refused. It was the right decision, for a month later, Buchan scored five goals in a 7-0 demolition of Liverpool, and in the return match at the end of the season, netted a hat-trick in a 5-2 win at Anfield!

The club trainer Billy Williams looked after him loyally and even made him give up cigarettes through the expediency of presenting him with a pipe - the pipe which later became so familiar an aspect of his public image.

His first England cap came on 15 February 1913 against Ireland in Belfast, with Mordue at his side and Cuggy behind him. It was a disastrous game for England, Ireland beating them for the first time ever, 2-1. Buchan however, headed the English goal after ten minutes. The three Sunderland players were dropped after the Irish match - despite the fact that the club came within an ace of the 'double' that season. Buchan hit one more hat-trick for the club before the Great War came, in a 5-0 home win over Tottenham Hotspur on the last day of league football before the hostilities.

Buchan went into the Grenadier Guards and four vital years were cut out of his career. He was an NCO in the trenches, and was brought back in 1918 to take a commission. On his return to England and football he played his victory game against Wales, partnered on the wing by the great Middlesex cricketer Patsy Hendren. He became a teacher for a time, and found it a strain, then opened a sports outfitters and went on playing for Sunderland until the summer of 1925.

After netting four goals in a 6-2 first round FA Cup win over Hull City in January 1920, he scored another four goals against Bolton Wanderers (Home 5-1) and a hat-trick in a 5-3 home defeat by Sheffield United in 1922-23, his most successful season for the club in terms of goals scored. In 1923-24 he scored hat-tricks in victories over Manchester City (Home 5-2) and Blackburn Rovers (Home 5-1) but the great pre-war Sunderland team had disintegrated, and in May 1925 after scoring 224 goals in 413 League and Cup games, he joined Arsenal.

The London club agreed to pay an initial £2,000 for Buchan's services, plus £100 for every goal he scored during his first season at Highbury. Herbert Chapman made him captain and he led Arsenal to their first-ever FA Cup Final against Cardiff City in 1927.

Charlie Buchan was at heart a traditionalist and an establishment man, a schoolmaster who gladly used the cane, and a brave soldier in the First World War.

BUCKLEY, MICK

A schoolboy start in his home-town of Manchester, Mick Buckley received offers from both City and United but surprised everyone by deciding to opt for Everton. He worked his way through the ranks to make his first team debut in a 2-2 draw at home to Wolverhampton Wanderers in March 1972. He was a member of the England Youth side that won the 'Little World Cup' in Spain later that year and went on to make two appearances for the England Under-23 side.

After a loan spell at Queen's Park Rangers, Buckley who had made 156 first team appearances for Everton, joined Sunderland in the summer of 1978 for a fee of £60,000.

His first game in Sunderland colours came in a 3-1 home win over Preston North End on 2 September 1978. Though he always gave 100% effort, he failed in his early days at Roker Park to match the performances he had produced for Everton. However, over the next five seasons he appeared in 137 games and endeared himself to Sunderland supporters when he scored the only goal of the game against Manchester City on the final day of the 1981-82 season that kept the Wearsiders in the top flight.

He left Sunderland in August 1983 and joined Hartlepool United as a non-contract player before later playing for Carlisle United and Middlesbrough.

Mick Buckley

BURBANKS, TED

Winger Ted Burbanks played his early football with Doncaster YMCA, Thorne and Denaby United before joining Sunderland in February 1935. He played his first game for the Wearsiders in April 1935, scoring their goal in a 1-1 home draw against Portsmouth. Though not a prolific scorer, he did find the net in Sunderland's 1937 FA Cup Final victory over Preston North End. Further success came to the left-winger during the Second World War when he 'guested' for Blackpool when they won the League (North) Cup in 1943 and beat Arsenal in a play-off against the Southern winners. When league football resumed in 1946-47, Burbanks was one of only three Sunderland players to have represented the club before the hostilities. He went on to score 29 goals in 155 games before in June 1948 he became Raich Carter's first major signing as manager of Hull City.

At Boothferry Park, his incisive running and ball skills added a new dimension to the Tigers' attack and in 1948-49 the Yorkshire club won the Third Division (North) championship. He continued to display his skills at Hull until the summer of 1953 when he joined Leeds United.

He became the oldest man to play for the Elland Road club when he captained the side in his final game in league football against Hull on 24 April 1954 - three weeks after his 41st birthday.

BUTCHER, TERRY

A commanding and competitive central defender, Terry Butcher began his Football League career with Ipswich Town where he established himself as a first team regular in 1978-79.

In 1980, Butcher won his first full cap for England when he played against Australia after winning honours at Under-21 and 'B' international level. Later that season, he helped Ipswich to a UEFA Cup Final victory over AZ67 Alkmaar and as runners-up in the First Division. He continued to be a mainstay of the Portman Road club's defence and in 1982-83 was ever-present. When Mick Mills left for Southampton, Butcher became captain, but in the summer of 1986, after making 344 first team appearances, he left to join Glasgow Rangers for a fee of £725,000.

At Ibrox Park he won three Scottish Premier League Championship medals, three Scottish League Cup winners' medals and a Scottish Cup runners-up medal.

Butcher, who won 77 caps for his country, played in three World Cup finals, including skippering them to the semi-final against West Germany in 1990.

In 1990 he joined Coventry City as player-manager but lost his job when he refused to negotiate a new 'manager only' contract after the chairman felt he should take a cut in salary as he was suffering from a long-term injury.

Following the sacking of Malcolm Crosby, Butcher became player-manager of Sunderland after joining the club in the summer of 1992. He made his debut in a 1-0 defeat at Swindon Town on the opening day of the 1992-93 season and appeared in 37 games for the Wearsiders. His contract was terminated in November 1993 and he now runs the 'The Old Manor Hotel' in Bridge of Allen near Stirling, though he still makes regular commentaries on Sky Television.

Sunderland's full league record under Terry Butcher is:

P	W	D	L	F	A
38	10	7	21	38	53

BUTLER, JOE

After beginning his working life as a miner, goalkeeper Joe Butler joined Stockport County in 1898, though he did not make a first team appearance until 1900. However, after securing a regular place in the County side, he became one of the most popular players in the club's history. He remained with Stockport following their fall from the Football League, helping them to win the Lancashire Combination and celebrating their success by converting a penalty in their penultimate game in 1904-05. Surprisingly, following County's successful application to the Second Division, Butler moved to Clapton Orient having made exactly 100 league appearances. After less than a year with Clapton, he returned to Edgeley Park and stayed for two more years before joining Glossop.

He spent four years with the Derbyshire club without missing a game although after making 152 consecutive appearances, he was suspended for the whole of the 1911-12 season following an incident in a game against Chelsea.

On his return from suspension he joined Sunderland and made his debut in a 2-0 defeat at Chelsea on 5 October 1912. This became Butler's most successful season as he won a First Division championship medal and an FA Cup runners-up medal, keeping 16 clean sheets in 42 games. After appearing in 80 consecutive League and Cup games from his debut, he joined Lincoln City before returning to Stockport County for a third time to play in the club's wartime games.

BUXTON, MICK

Mick Buxton appeared in only a few league games during his playing career with Burnley and Halifax Town but has since been involved in the game both as a coach and a manager.

After representing Sunderland Schoolboys, he joined Burnley where he was involved in two successive Central League Championship campaigns, but five years after making his first team debut he joined Halifax, immediately helping the Shaymen win promotion to the Third Division. After two broken legs, his playing career ended in 1971 and he joined the Halifax coaching staff, later coaching at Watford, Mansfield, Barnsley and Southend United. After being appointed first team coach at Huddersfield Town, he took over as manager. In 1980, the Terriers won the Fourth Division championship and another promotion followed in 1983 but at Christmas 1984, he was sacked with Huddersfield lying bottom of the Second Division.

He was appointed manager of Scunthorpe United in 1987 and guided them to the Fourth Division play-offs in 1988 and 1989 but after promotion eluded them, he was dismissed.

After a spell on Sunderland's coaching staff under Terry Butcher he became caretaker manager in November 1993 and was appointed manager in April 1994. Just a year later, he was replaced by Peter Reid.

He was appointed Scunthorpe's manager for a second time in April 1996 but was replaced by Brian Laws ten months later.

Sunderland's full league record under Mick Buxton is:

P	W	D	L	F	A
68	23	21	24	72	70

C

CAMPBELL, JOHNNY

One of the club's greatest ever goalscorers, Johnny Campbell joined Sunderland from Renton in 1889 and after appearing in an FA Cup game during the 1889-90 season, made his league debut in the 3-2 home defeat by Burnley in the club's inaugural season in the Football League.

Campbell had the honour of scoring the club's first hat-trick in the Football League when he in fact netted four of Sunderland's goals in a 5-2 win at Bolton Wanderers. He followed this up later in the season with a hat-trick in a 5-1 home win over Aston Villa and ended the campaign as the club's leading scorer with 23 goals in 26 games. In 1891-92, Campbell had his most successful season in terms of goals scored when he found the net 35 times in 29 games. Included in this total were four goals in a 6-1 home win over Blackburn Rovers and hat-tricks against West Bromwich Albion (Home 4-0), Darwen (Away 7-1) and Accrington (Away 3-1) as Sunderland went on to win the League Championship for the first time.

When the club retained the title the following season, Campbell was again the leading scorer with 31 goals in 30 games including four hat-tricks against West Bromwich Albion (Home 8-1) Newton Heath (Away 5-0) and in both matches against Accrington (Home 4-2 and Away 6-1). After relinquishing his position as the club's leading scorer to Jimmy Millar in 1893-94, he was back to his best the following season as the Wearsiders won the League Championship for the third time in four seasons.

Though he failed to score a hat-trick in his total of 21 goals, he did so the following season in a 7-1 home defeat of West Bromwich Albion, his third against the Baggies.

Campbell had scored 150 goals in 215 League and Cup games when he left the club in 1897 to join neighbours and rivals Newcastle United in a joint deal with John Harvey for £40. Although he was now classed as a veteran, he gave the Magpies much needed experience and composure.

CAMPBELL, ROBERT

Robert Campbell replaced Tom Watson as Sunderland's secretary-manager in August 1896 but it took the club until the ninth game of the season before they recorded their first win - a 4-3 home defeat of Tom Watson's new club, Liverpool! At the end of his first season in charge, Sunderland were in 15th position out of the 16 clubs.

As there was no automatic promotion or relegation at this time, a series of Test matches were arranged to decide which teams would play in which divisions the following season. Campbell piloted the club through these Test matches to retain their First Division status.

The following season of 1897-98 saw Sunderland finish the campaign as runners-up to Sheffield United, five points adrift of the champions. At the end of the 1898-99 season in which Sunderland finished seventh out of 18 clubs, Campbell left the club to become manager of Bristol City.

Under his managership, Bristol City were elected to the Football League but he left the club after two years after a disagreement over a huge wage bill. After a couple of years out of the game, he took charge at Bradford City and in his two seasons at the club, put them on a firm footing as they finished in the top half of the Second Division. In 1905 he left the club by mutual consent, moving to Scotland where he made a name for himself lecturing on football.

Sunderland's full league record under Robert Campbell is:

P	W	D	L	F	A
94	38	20	36	118	118

CAPACITY

The total capacity of the Stadium of Light in 1998-99 was 41,590.

CAPS
The most capped player in the club's history is Charlie Hurley, who won 38 caps for the Republic of Ireland.

CAPS (ENGLAND)
The first Sunderland player to be capped by England was Tom Porteous when he played against Wales in 1891. The most capped player is Dave Watson with 14 caps.

CAPS (NORTHERN IRELAND)
The first Sunderland player to be capped by Northern Ireland was Harry Buckle when he played against England in 1904. The most capped player is Martin Harvey with 34 caps.

CAPS (REPUBLIC OF IRELAND)
The first Sunderland player to be capped by the Republic of Ireland was John Feenan when he played against Switzerland in 1937. The most capped player is Charlie Hurley with 38 caps.

CAPS (SCOTLAND)
The first Sunderland player to be capped by Scotland was Ned Doig when he played against England in 1896. The most capped player is Jim Baxter with 10 caps.

CAPS (WALES)
The first Sunderland player to be capped by Wales was Leigh Roose when he played against England in 1908. The most capped player is Andy Melville with 17 caps.

CAPTAINS
Among the many players who have captained the club are Robert Singleton who was elected the club's first captain at the inaugural meeting of 'The Sunderland and District Reachers' Association Football Club' in October 1879. Scottish international Hugh Wilson who possessed an exceptionally long throw-in captained the club in their early years in the Football League as they won the League Championship three times in four seasons between 1891-92 and 1894-95. Charlie Thomson was a no-nonsense centre-half who led Sunderland to the League Championship in 1912-13 and to the FA Cup Final where they lost 1-0 to Aston Villa.

Another Scottish international, wing-half Alex Hastings captained the Wearsiders to the League title in 1935-36 whilst it was Raich Carter who skippered the side in the FA Cup Final at Wembley the following season. When Sunderland won the FA Cup for a second time in 1973, it was Bobby Kerr who led them to victory over First Division Leeds United.

When Sunderland won the First Division Championship in 1995-96 with a total of 83 points, they were captained by the irrepressible Kevin Ball, who is still producing outstanding performances in the Sunderland side after well over 300 first team appearances. He led the team to the First Division Championship again in 1998-99 when the Wearsiders amassed 105 points.

CARTER, RAICH

His father was 'Toddler' Carter, a winger with Port Vale, Fulham and Southampton, who tragically died of a brain tumour when Raich was just 14, having never seen his son play.

Raich Carter caught the selectors' attention early and after appearing for Sunderland boys, playing in the same distinguished England Schoolboys team as Len Goulden and Cliff Bastin. An excellent all-round athlete, he could have been almost as successful as a cricketer, but with Durham not having first-class status then, it would have meant a move and a wait.

After leaving school, he became an errand boy and then apprentice electrician but his heart was not in electrical engineering and he jumped at the chance of a trial with Leicester City. Playing out of position, he had a poor game and was told he was too small for professional football. The following season he sought a trial with Sunderland and though he signed amateur forms for the Wearsiders, he was not used again after his trial. Forgetting that he was still technically on Sunderland's books, he was given the chance of a trial with Huddersfield Town. This led to a row between the managers of the two clubs but gave Carter his chance. He played a number of games in Sunderland's reserve side in the North Eastern League before being offered professional terms.

He eventually made his league debut at Sheffield Wednesday on 15 October 1932 and two games later on his home debut, scored his first league goal for the club in a 7-4 win over Bolton Wanderers.

In 1933-34, Carter scored his first hat-trick for the club in a 6-0 home win over Tottenham Hotspur. The following season, he and Bob Gurney were both selected for the full international trial to be played at Roker Park. Carter scored four goals and Gurney two as The Rest beat England 7-1.

This led to him winning the first of 13 full caps when he played against Scotland at Wembley in April 1934.

The brilliance of Carter's performances for Sunderland, where he became a very young captain, helped the club win the League Championship in 1935-36. That season he scored 31 goals in 39 league games including four goals in a 6-1 defeat of West Bromwich Albion. The following season he scored another hat-trick in a 4-1 win over Middlesbrough and led Sunderland to their first ever FA Cup Final triumph.

In the final against Preston North End, things were going badly and at half-time, Sunderland went in a goal behind. But in the second-half, Carter and his cleverly varied passes began to call the tune. Sunderland equalised, Carter put them ahead and eventually his side won 3-1.

The Second World War brought an abrupt end to football and as with so many, robbed Raich Carter of his best years. Bomb damage to the family home in Sunderland led to a move to Derby and it was at the Baseball Ground where Carter chose to play his wartime football. After the hostilities had ended, Carter who scored 130 goals in 279 League and Cup games, joined County on a permanent basis.

With the Rams he went on to win another FA Cup winners' medal, the only player to gain such a medal both before and after the war.

Before long, a number of clubs began to show an interest in him and he stepped down to the Third Division with Hull City. Almost immediately he found himself player-manager as the Tigers' boss Frank Buckley moved on. He took Hull to a quarter-final appearance against Manchester United and to promotion to the Second Division. After his success with Hull and a spell with Cork Athletic, Carter became manager of Leeds United. He later took charge at Mansfield Town and Middlesbrough but after the then Ayresome Park club were relegated to the Third Division, he was dismissed.

CENTURIES

Nine individual players have scored 100 or more league goals for Sunderland. Charlie Buchan is the greatest goalscorer with 209 strikes in his career in the north-east (1911-1925). The other centurions are Bob Gurney (205); Dave Halliday (153); George Holley (145); Johnny Campbell (133); Raich Carter (121); Arthur Bridgett (111); Johnny Millar (106); and Patsy Gallacher (101).

Charlie Thomson holds the club record for the most consecutive league appearances - 133. Other players to have made over 100 consecutive league appearances during their careers are George Mulhall (114); Darius Kubicki (112); Andrew McAllister (106); Bert Davis (104); and Barry Siddall (103).

CHAIRMEN

Below is a full list of the club's chairmen with the years of their terms of office:

James Henderson	1895-1903	Col John Turnbull	1957-1958
Sinclair Todd	1903-1904	Stanley Ritson	1958-1960
Frederick Taylor	1904-1913	Syd Collings	1960-1968
Samuel Wilson	1913-1921	Jack Parker	1968-1971
William Bell	1921-1930	Keith Collings	1971-1980
Sir Walter Raine	1930-1938	Sir Tom Cowie	1980-1986
Duncan White	1938-1940	Bob Murray	1986-1993
Col Joseph Prior	1940-1949	John Featherstone	1993-1995
Edward Ditchburn	1949-1957	Bob Murray	1995-

CHAMPIONSHIPS

Sunderland have won a divisional League Championship on nine occasions.

The first time was in 1891-92 in what was only the club's second season in the Football League. After beating Wolves 5-2 on the opening day of the season, a match in which Jimmy Millar scored a hat-trick, the Wearsiders lost their next three matches. However, out of their next 22 games, they won 20 including 13 consecutive games between 14 November 1891 and 2 April 1892 - a club record. They ended the season with 42 points, five points clear of runners-up Preston North End.

The club retained the title the following season, after a good start saw them win seven of their first eight fixtures. They suffered only four defeats throughout the season and scored 100 goals in their 30 games. After finishing runners-up in 1893-94, Sunderland won the title for a third time in four seasons in 1894-95 when four players managed to get in double figures in terms of goals scored.

Sunderland won their fourth League Championship in 1901-02, though to be fair, their results compared to the other seasons when they had won the title, were not memorable.

When the Wearsiders won the League Championship in 1912-13 they secured 54 points, beating the existing points record for a League Championship-winning side by one point. They ended the season four points ahead of runners-up Aston Villa, who beat Sunderland in the FA Cup Final to prevent the Wearsiders completing a League and Cup double.

The club had to wait a further 19 Football League seasons before the Championship trophy returned to Roker Park. After a 3-1 defeat at Arsenal on the opening day of the season, the Wearsiders took 11 points from their next six matches including a 7-2 win over Blackburn Rovers. Later in the season they beat Bolton Wanderers 7-2 with Bob Gurney scoring five of the goals.

The club scored 109 league goals during that campaign, 20 more than any other club and finished eight points clear of runners-up Derby County.

After relegation in 1957-58, the club spent six seasons in the Second Division before returning to the top flight as runners-up to Leeds United in 1963-64. They returned to the Second Division six seasons later and won the Championship in 1975-76. They were undefeated at home, dropping only two points, one each to Bristol City and Bristol Rovers!

After only one season in the top flight, Sunderland were relegated to the Second Division and though they were promoted as runners-up to Leicester City in 1979-80, within five seasons they were back in Division Two. After losing in the play-offs in 1986-87, Sunderland found themselves in the Third Division for the first time in their history.

After winning their first-ever game in this Division 1-0 at Brentford, the club led the table for most of the season and won the Championship with a record 93 points.

Sunderland won the First Division in 1995-96 and established a club record of being unbeaten in 18 matches and 26 clean sheets. They finished four points ahead of runners-up Derby County to win the First Division championship and promotion to the Premier League.

Despite being relegated after just one season in the top flight, the Wearsiders won the First Division title again in 1998-99. They were unbeaten in their first 18 matches and ended the campaign with just three defeats and a total of 105 points.

CHARITY SHIELD
Sunderland have appeared twice in the FA Charity Shield - in 1936 as League Champions and in 1937 as FA Cup winners. The results were as follows:

1936	Sunderland 2 Arsenal 1	at Roker Park
1937	Manchester City 2 Sunderland 0	at Maine Road

CHISHOLM, GORDON

Glasgow-born central defender Gordon Chisholm was drafted into the Sunderland side for the opening game of the 1978-79 season and starred in a 1-0 home win over Charlton Athletic.

In his early days with the club he was more of a utility player and filled a variety of positions, scoring his first goal towards the end of his first season in the team in a 3-0 home defeat of Notts County. He was a valuable member of the Wearsiders' squad for seven seasons, appearing in 248 games and scoring 17 goals.

After the club were relegated to the Second Division at the end of the 1984-85 season, Chisholm appeared in just one game for the Wearsiders before being allowed to leave Roker Park and return to his native Scotland to join Hibernian for a fee of £30,000.

Gordon Chisholm

CHISHOLM, KEN

Ken Chisholm was a fighter pilot during the Second World War. He joined Queen's Park in 1945 and the following year turned out for Scotland in a Victory international against Northern Ireland. He left Hampden Park in 1946 for Partick Thistle and the legendary Major Frank Buckley, manager of Leeds United, signed him from Partick in January 1948.

He stayed at Elland Road for less than a year before moving to Leicester City with whom he won his only honour, an FA Cup runners-up medal in 1949.

In March 1950 he signed for Coventry City and soon became a great favourite at Highfield Road. In 1950-51, his only complete season with the Sky Blues, he netted 24 goals, most of them before Christmas. Sold to Cardiff City, he helped the Bluebirds win promotion to the First Division and in his first two seasons in the top flight, he was the club's leading scorer.

He joined Sunderland at the end of December 1953 and made his debut for the Wearsiders on New Year's Day 1954 in a 2-0 home win over Aston Villa. The following season he was the club's leading scorer with 22 goals in 43 games including a hat-trick in a 4-3 home win over Manchester United. He went on to score 37 goals in 86 games before leaving Roker Park to join Workington and later became Glentoran's player-manager.

Chisholm was one of the players involved in the Sunderland illegal payments scandal of the 1950s. He was suspended *sine die* for refusing to answer the investigating committee's questions. Subsequently he admitted receiving illegal payments and forfeited his benefit qualification terms.

CLARK, LEE

One of the most talented of Newcastle United's crop of youngsters, he made his debut for the Magpies as a substitute at Bristol City in September 1990 and was later selected by manager Ossie Ardilles for the last nine games of the season. When Ardilles lost his job, new manager Kevin Keegan replaced the youngsters, Clark included, with more experienced new signings.

By 1992-93 he was back in the Newcastle side and was voted the north-east's 'Footballer of the Year' for some outstanding performances as United won the First Division Championship. He was the only ever-present, playing in all 58 competitive matches and scoring an invaluable ten goals. Over the next four seasons, Clark was a virtual ever-present until the arrival of David Batty. Though he did win a return to the Newcastle side, the wealth of talent at St James' Park led to his first team opportunities being limited and after scoring 27 goals in 240 games, he left the Magpies in June 1997, joining Sunderland for a £2.5 million fee.

After making his debut in a 2-0 defeat at Sheffield United on the opening day of the 1997-98 season, he went on to be an ever-present, scoring 13 goals including doubles against Stoke City and Tranmere Rovers. Also in 1997-98 in the absence of Kevin Ball, 'Clarkie' was awarded the captaincy and was named in the PFA Division One Select XI.

The influential midfielder broke his leg in the opening game of the 1998-99 season as Sunderland beat Queen's Park Rangers 1-0, but bounced back to help the Wearsiders win the First Division Championship.

CLARKE, JEFF

Born in Pontefract, centre-half Jeff Clarke began his career with Manchester City, but after just 13 league appearances for the Maine Road club, he joined Sunderland in the summer of 1975 for a fee of £175,000.

He played his first game for the club in a 2-1 home win over Chelsea on the opening day of the 1975-76 campaign and over the next six seasons, this commanding central defensive figure was the mainstay of the

Jeff Clarke

Sunderland side. He won a Second Division Championship medal in his first season with the Wearsiders and was a member of the side that again won promotion to the top flight in 1979-80. Clarke had played in 217 League and Cup games for Sunderland when he was surprisingly given a free transfer and joined rivals Newcastle United in July 1982.

The Yorkshireman bolstered the Magpies' defence and was with the St James' Park club for four seasons until an injury ended his playing days with them. He later remained associated with United, working in the club's junior development programme and as reserve team coach.

CLEAN SHEET

This is the colloquial expression used to describe a goalkeeper's performance when he does not concede a goal. Jim Montgomery has kept 20 clean sheets in a season on two occasions. In 1963-64 he was ever-present as the club won promotion to the First Division and in 1974-75 he achieved the feat playing in 40 matches. In 1993-94, Alec Chamberlain kept 19 clean sheets in 43 league games along with another three in cup matches.

CLOUGH, BRIAN

One of nine children, Brian Clough worked as a clerk with ICI whilst playing for Billingham Synthonia and Great Broughton before joining Middlesbrough. He was one of the greatest of marksmen with 204 goals in 222 appearances for 'Boro and was the leading goalscorer in the Second Division for three seasons on the trot and scored 40 goals or more every season from 1956 to 1960.

In July 1961 he moved to Sunderland for a fee of £45,000 and made his debut for the Wearsiders at Walsall on the opening day of the 1961-62 season, scoring a goal in a 4-3 defeat. That season Clough top scored with 29 goals in 34 league games and netted four hat-tricks in victories over Bury (Home 3-0) Plymouth Argyle (Home 5-0) Swansea Town (Home 7-2) and Huddersfield Town (Home 3-1). He also scored a hat-trick in the 5-2 League Cup win over Walsall at Roker Park to take his season's total to 34 goals in 43 matches.

In 1962-63, Clough had scored 28 goals in 28 games including hat-tricks against Southampton (Away 4-2) and Grimsby Town (Home 6-2) when he chased a ball into the Bury penalty area on Boxing Day and collided with Chris Harker the Shakers' 'keeper. The injury he received virtually ended his playing career. He tried to make a comeback but when he realised it was a hopeless cause, he retired from playing after scoring 63 goals in 74 games for the Wearsiders. He failed to score in either of his two internationals for England but would probably have won many more caps playing for a more fashionable southern club.

After a spell on Sunderland's coaching staff, he took his first steps in management with Hartlepool United where Peter Taylor joined him. The two moved to Derby County and led the Rams to the Second Division Championship. After a number of major signings, County won the League Championship for the first time in their history in 1971-72. The following season they reached the semi-finals of the European Cup before losing to Juventus.

Following a dispute with Derby chairman Sam Longson, Clough and Taylor accepted an offer to manage Third Division Brighton. Clough left the south coast club in July 1974 and took over at Leeds United the following month, yet after only 44 days in charge, he was sacked!

He was not out of work for long, and in January 1975 became manager of Nottingham Forest. Over the next 18 years he was to produce some golden moments for the City Ground club, including a League Championship, four League Cup wins and two European Cup successes.

There is no doubt that Brian Clough is one of the greatest managers of all time. In May 1993 amidst a lot of bad publicity, he decided to retire, having won just about everything there is to win.

CLUNAS, BILLY

Wing-half Billy Clunas joined the Wearsiders from St Mirren in November 1923 and made his debut within two days of signing for the club in a 2-1 home win over Huddersfield Town. At the end of his first season with the club in which he appeared in 21 games, he won his first full cap for Scotland when he played against England at Wembley. He gave a commanding performance in the middle of the park as the Scots drew 1-1. His second cap followed two seasons later when he played against Wales.

Though not a prolific scorer, his best season in terms of goals scored was 1928-29 when he netted 12 in 37 league games including doubles against Huddersfield Town (Home 4-1) Leeds United (Away 3-0) and Manchester City (Home 3-1).

He went on to score 44 goals in 272 League and Cup games for Sunderland before leaving Roker Park in the summer of 1931 to return to Scotland to play for Morton.

COCHRANE, JOHNNY

In his younger days, Johnny Cochrane had played football for Paisley Grammar School, Johnston Thistle, Elderslie Amateurs and St Johnstone before taking up secretarial duties with the latter club in 1912.

In 1916 he became manager of St Mirren and in his tenth year with the club he led them to fourth place in the Scottish League and to victory over Celtic in the final of the Scottish Cup.

After the club had failed in their attempts to secure the services of both George Jobey and Major Frank Buckley as replacement for manager Robert Kyle, they turned to their third choice, Johnny Cochrane.

On his arrival at Roker Park, he was soon active in the transfer market, buying Adam McClean and Tom McInally. These signings helped the club finish fourth in Division One in Cochrane's first season.

Gradually he began to produce a side which was more than capable of challenging for the League Championship, playing entertaining football and scoring plenty of goals. In 1934-35 the Wearsiders finished runners-up to Arsenal but the following season took the title outright to break the Gunners' hold on the trophy. Sunderland were in fact eight points clear of Derby County their nearest rivals and scored 109 goals. A year later, the Reds won the FA Cup beating Preston North End 3-1 in the Wembley final. The club almost returned to Wembley again the following year but lost to Huddersfield Town in the semi-finals.

Johnny Cochrane, who was well known for his laid back approach left Roker Park in March 1939 to take charge of Reading but lasted only 13 days before resigning!

Sunderland's full league record under Johnny Cochrane is:

P	W	D	L	F	A
452	190	101	161	866	785

COLOURS

The famous red and white stripes made their first appearance when Sunderland began the 1886-87 season with a home match against a Notts and District XI which the Wearsiders won 1-0.

The first time the club changed their colours was in unusual circumstances. On 27 January 1951, Sunderland met Southampton at Roker Park in an FA Cup match. Because of the colour clash and Southampton not having brought a change of kit, Sunderland borrowed Newcastle

United's black and white striped shirts. It didn't affect their game as they beat the south coast club 2-0.

In 1961-62 the club changed their traditional black shorts for white ones, along with new red and white socks. However, when Bob Stokoe was appointed manager in November 1972, his first act was to change the club's colours back to the original black shorts - a most popular move with the supporters!

At the beginning of the 1981-82 season, the club decided to have a completely new style of strip, wearing shirts with a narrow red stripe on a white background, red shorts and socks. Two seasons later, the club reverted to the more acceptable red and white stripes and black shorts, though slightly updated from previous strips.

The club's present colours are red and white striped shirts, black shorts, black stockings with a red turnover. The club's change colours are navy blue shirts with a red and white hoop across the chest, navy shorts and stockings with a red and white trim.

CONNOR, JIMMY

Left-winger Jimmy Connor joined Sunderland from Scottish League club St Mirren in the summer of 1930 and played his first game for the club in a 3-3 home draw against Manchester City on the opening day of the 1930-31 season. He ended the campaign with 17 goals in 47 games, the most successful of his nine seasons at Roker Park in terms of goals scored.

A Scottish international, winning the first of his four caps against France in 1930, he missed very few games for the Wearsiders and in 1935-36 when the club won the League Championship, he was ever-present. He went on to appear in 284 League and Cup games, scoring 61 goals and though he never scored a hat-trick, he did net nine doubles.

He played the last of his games in Sunderland's colours in an FA Cup fifth round second replay against Blackburn Rovers at Hillsborough in February 1939, a game which the Wearsiders lost 1-0, after which he hung up his boots.

CONSECUTIVE HOME GAMES

Sunderland have played an extraordinary intense sequence of five home games in succession on four occasions. In 1927-28 they played five games in the space of just 19 days. After beating Arsenal 5-1, a match in which Bob Gurney scored a hat-trick, they drew 1-1 with Newcastle United and played out a goalless draw with Tottenham Hotspur before losing 2-0 to Everton and 1-0 to Derby County.

CONSECUTIVE SCORING - LONGEST SEQUENCE

Arthur Bridgett, Dave Halliday and Raich Carter hold the club record for consecutive scoring in the Football League, the three players being on target in eight consecutive games. Their records are as follows:

Arthur Bridgett (1906-07)

Everton (Away 1-4)	1 goal
Middlesbrough (Home 4-2)	2 goals
Arsenal (Home 2-3)	1 goal
Sheff Wed (Away 1-2)	1 goal
Bury (Home 3-5)	1 goal
Notts County (Home 3-1)	1 goal
Manchester City (Away 3-2)	1 goal
Leicester Fosse (Home 4-1)	1 goal

Dave Halliday (1927-28)

Portsmouth (Home 3-3)	1 goal
West Ham Utd (Away 4-2)	2 goals
Leicester City (Away 3-3)	2 goals
Birmingham (Home 4-2)	1 goal
Liverpool (Home 2-1)	1 goal
Arsenal (Away 1-2)	1 goal
Burnley (Home 2-3)	1 goal
Bury (Away 3-5)	3 goal

Raich Carter (1935-36)

Wolves (Away 4-3)	2 goals
Sheff Wed (Home 5-1)	2 goals
Portsmouth (Away 2-2)	2 goals
Preston N.E.(Home 4-2)	1 goal
Brentford (Away 5-1)	1 goal
Middlesbrough (Home 2-1)	2 goals
Everton (Away 3-0)	1 goal
Bolton Wands (Home 7-2)	1 goal

CRESSWELL, WARNEY

One of the game's classiest defenders Warney Cresswell began his career with South Shields where he won an international cap against Wales in 1921. When he left to join Sunderland in 1922 for £5,500, it was a British record.

He made his debut for the Wearsiders in a 1-0 home win over Sheffield United on 4 March 1922 and went on to be a first team regular in the Sunderland side for the next six seasons, appearing in 190 League and Cup games. He also made five further appearances at full international level before leaving Roker Park in February 1927 to sign for Everton.

Despite a disastrous debut for the Goodison Park club in a 6-2 defeat at Leicester City, he retained his place in the side and over the next ten seasons was a regular member of an Everton side that won two League Championships, the FA Cup and the Second Division championship. In 1929 he played for England against Northern Ireland to win his seventh cap and went on to appear in 306 League and Cup games for the Toffees before leaving the club in 1936.

After a spell as manager-coach of Port Vale, he was appointed manager of Northampton Town, a position he held for two years before taking charge at non-League Dartford.

CRICKETERS

Sunderland have had two players who were cricketers of real note. Walter Keeton who joined the club from Grantham Town in October 1930, played just 12 games for the club in two seasons at Roker Park. His only goal for the Wearsiders came in a 3-0 win at West Ham United in April 1931. Keeton was a very good county opening batsman, making a magnificent contribution to Nottinghamshire cricket. He scored 23,744 runs at an average of 40.18 and a top score of 312 not out against Middlesex in 1939. Exceeding 1000 runs in a season 12 times, including 2,000 on six occasions, he twice scored three hundreds in consecutive innings and played for England in two Test matches.

Willie Watson was a tenacious left-half who joined Sunderland from Huddersfield Town in April 1946. The winner of four international caps for England, he scored 16 goals in 223 League and Cup games for the Wearsiders before leaving to join Halifax Town. After making his Test debut against South Africa at Trent Bridge in 1951, Watson appeared in six more Tests before playing his first against Australia at Lord's in 1953.

At the start of the final day, England looked doomed. His last-ditch stand with Trevor Bailey was one of Test cricket's most heroic feats. The pair survived for 257 minutes and Watson who scored 109 went on to help England win the series and regain the Ashes. After scoring 14,049 runs for Yorkshire at 38.28, he moved to Leicestershire as captain and assistant-secretary prior to becoming a Test selector.

CROSBY, MALCOLM

Malcolm Crosby played his football with Aldershot and York City making 427 league appearances for the two clubs and helping them both win promotion.

After hanging up his boots he became youth team coach at Sunderland before becoming caretaker manager following the sacking of Denis Smith. He led the Wearsiders to an FA Cup Final in 1992 despite the club struggling against relegation to the Third Division. In fact, it was not until just before the Cup Final that the board offered him the job on a permanent basis.

Sunderland lost the final to Liverpool but retained their Second Division status. Crosby was relieved of his duties in February 1993, hearing the news over the telephone.

Sunderland's full league record under Malcolm Crosby is:

P	W	D	L	F	A
46	14	12	20	56	66

CROSSAN, JOHNNY

Johnny Crossan first hit the headlines whilst an amateur with Irish League club, Coleraine, when he was alleged to have been paid. Peter Doherty brought him to England to sign for Bristol City but when the Irishman's registration forms were sent to the Football League for approval, they were refused and Crossan was later banned from playing in England. He then signed for the Dutch League club Sparta Rotterdam before later playing for the Belgian League champions Standard Liege.

When the Football League ban was eventually lifted, Crossan joined Sunderland in October 1962 for a fee of £26,700. He made his debut in a 6-2 home win over Grimsby Town and though he failed to get on the scoresheet, it wasn't long before he scored the first of two hat-tricks for the club in a 3-2 win at Walsall in March 1963. His second came at the end of the season in a 4-0 home win over Southampton. During the club's promotion-winning season of 1963-64, Crossan who was ever-present, scored 22 goals including five 'doubles' and another five goals in six FA Cup games. Midway through the 1964-65 season, Crossan who had scored 48 goals in 99 games left Roker Park to sign for Manchester City for a fee of £40,000.

He skippered City back to the First Division but after losing his place to Colin Bell he joined Middlesbrough for £35,000 - 'Boro's record fee. Capped

24 times by Northern Ireland, Crossan suffered from insomnia and received hospital treatment during his time at Ayresome Park before leaving to return to Belgium where he ended his career with Tongren FC.

CROWD TROUBLE

However unwelcome, crowd disturbances are far from a modern phenomenon at major football matches.

Behaviour at Roker Park and The Stadium of Light has usually been of a high standard and though Sunderland supporters are well renowned for voicing their opinions at suspect referees, the occasions when their demonstrations boil over beyond the verbal are very rare indeed. However, a number of such occasions did occur in the club's early days.

It was at St James' Park, not Roker Park in the 'derby' match against Newcastle United in 1901 that fighting broke out between rival supporters in a near 50,000 crowd. The corner flags and goal-posts were torn down, the pitch was turned into a ploughed field and the match was abandoned without a start being made. It happened on Good Friday!

In March 1903, Sunderland lost 1-0 at home to Sheffield Wednesday. The game finished on a sour note as some of the Sunderland fans stoned the referee as he left the ground. Sunderland were ordered to shut Roker Park for a week, but the defeat turned out to be a bigger punishment because it cost them the League title!

After those two incidents, there were a number of pitch invasions at Roker Park, one of which in 1909, a police horse was stabbed.

CUGGY, FRANK

Frank Cuggy was an attacking wing-half with superb ball control who delighted in the Scottish style of triangular play between wing-half, winger and inside-forward and along with Jackie Mordue and Charlie Buchan, was probably the finest exponent of this pattern.

Cuggy joined Sunderland from Willingham Athletic in March 1909 and made his first team debut at centre-half in a 3-2 defeat at Aston Villa in February 1910. After making three appearances in both 1909-10 and 1910-11, Cuggy established himself as a regular in the Sunderland side and in 1912-13 won a League Championship medal and played in all of the club's games as they reached that season's FA Cup Final, where they lost 1-0 to Aston Villa. His form during that season was so impressive that he won the first of two caps against Northern Ireland in Belfast but was on the losing side as England went down 2-1.

In 1919, he played in the majority of the club's Victory League games and appeared in 34 matches in 1919-20 as the club finished fifth in Division One in the first season of League football after the hostilities.

He went on to appear in 190 League and Cup games for the north-east club before leaving Roker Park in May 1921 to join Wallsend.

CUMMINS, STAN

Stan Cummins began his Football League career with Middlesbrough but in three years at Ayresome Park was never able to establish himself in the Teeside club's first team. He had scored nine goals in 44 league games when Sunderland paid £300,000 for his services in November 1979.

The diminutive midfielder scored on his debut in a 3-1 home win over Notts County and on 9 February 1980 scored four goals for the Wearsiders in a 5-0 defeat of Burnley. He ended his first season at Roker Park with 12 league goals in 26 games, helping the club regain their top flight status.

He was ever-present in 1980-81 and a first team regular for the next couple of seasons, when, having scored 32 goals in 146 games, he was allowed to join Crystal Palace on a free transfer. After a little over a year at Selhurst Park, Cummins returned to Sunderland but was unable to prevent the club from relegation to the Second Division, and at the end of that 1984-85 season in which he had appeared in a further 21 games without scoring, he left to join Minnesota Strikers in the NASL.

Stan Cummins

D

DANIEL, RAY

After playing for his home-town club Swansea during the latter part of the Second World War as an amateur, Daniel Ray was offered a chance at Highbury and signed for the Gunners in October 1946. His early days were spent with the reserves at Hendon, being groomed as a successor to ageing first team centre-half Leslie Compton. After National Service he made his first team debut for Arsenal in the 1948-49 season whilst Compton ended the season early to play cricket for Middlesex.

The Welsh selectors gave him an early chance whilst he was still in Arsenal's reserves against England in November 1950. Though Wales had no qualms in picking him, a regular Arsenal place did not come until 1951-52.

An FA Cup Final appearance came in 1952 against Newcastle United but in difficult circumstances, as he had only passed a late fitness test on a broken wrist which had been set in plaster. After a clash with Jackie Milburn, the partly knitted bone was broken again, leaving him to battle on in agony. In 1953, Arsenal won the League Championship but Daniel's adventurous play brought him into conflict with manager Tom Whittaker and in the summer of 1953 he was allowed to join Sunderland for £27,000.

His first game in the red and white stripes was against Charlton Athletic at The Valley on the opening day of the 1953-54 season, a game which Sunderland lost 5-3. Over the next four seasons, Daniel was a virtual ever-present, though by and large, he, along with the other great individuals such as Shackleton, Bingham and Ford failed to blend as a team. Allegations regarding illegal bonuses paid to various players were reported to the Football League and Daniel was amongst those suspended. It cost him a fine and several international caps, the last of his 21 appearances coming against Czechoslovakia in a World Cup game only days after the suspension had ended.

He later joined Cardiff City for a short spell before seeing his league career out with Swansea in 1960.

DAVENPORT, PETER

Birkenhead-born Peter Davenport began his footballing career as an amateur with Everton but in 1980 he was released. It was while playing for Cammel Laird FC that he began to attract the attention of Nottingham Forest and in January 1982 he joined the City Ground club.

He made a sensational start to his Forest career, scoring four goals in his five appearances at the end of the 1981-82 season, including a hat-trick in a 3-1 win over Ipswich Town. After a season in which he was hampered by injuries, he was the club's leading scorer for the next two terms and in September 1984 he hit his second hat-trick for the club in a 3-1 win over Sunderland. It was this form that led to him winning an England cap against the Republic of Ireland. In March 1986 after scoring 54 goals in 118 league games, he moved to Manchester United for £570,000. The move didn't work out for him and two years later he moved on to Middlesbrough for £700,000.

In 1990-91 he was back in the top flight with Sunderland and made a goalscoring debut in a 3-2 defeat at Norwich City on the opening day of the season. His early form with the club was good but a series of niggling injuries and a loss of form meant that he spent much of his time with the Wearsiders on the bench. More of a provider than a goalscorer, he found the net 18 times in 129 League and Cup appearances before moving to play for Airdrie, St Johnstone and Stockport County.

DAVIS, BERT

Bert Davis joined Sunderland from Bradford Park Avenue in April 1932 and made his debut for the Wearsiders in a 3-2 home win over Manchester City on the opening day of the 1932-33 season. During that season, Davis scored his only hat-trick for the club as Blackburn Rovers were beaten 4-2 in front of a Roker Park crowd of just 15,000. He was ever-present in season's 1933-34 and 1934-35, appearing in 104 consecutive league games. In 1935-36 as he had in the previous two seasons, the dependable forward scored 10 league goals but in this League Championship-winning season, his total came from just 25 games as he competed for the number seven shirt with Len Duns. He went on to score 40 goals in 163 League and Cup games before leaving Roker Park in December 1936 to join Leicester City.

DAVIS, DICKIE

An England Schoolboy international, centre-forward Dickie Davis joined his home-town club Birmingham and played for the club's youth team before joining Sunderland in May 1939. Due to the Second World War, he had to wait for the resumption of peacetime football before making his league debut for the Wearsiders in a 1-1 draw at Leeds United on 7 December 1946. A week later he scored Sunderland's goal on his home debut in a 4-1 defeat at the hands of Liverpool.

In 1947-48 he scored 12 goals in 26 league games and the following season netted the first of three hat-tricks for the club in a 3-1 win at Preston North End. In 1949-50 when Sunderland finished third in Division One, Davis was the club's top scorer with 25 goals in 34 games including hat-tricks against Derby County (Home 6-1) and Wolverhampton Wanderers (Away 3-1). He went on to score 79 goals in 154 first team outings before leaving Roker Park in the summer of 1954 to join Darlington. Davis scored 32 goals in 93 league games for the Quakers before leaving the first-class game.

DEATH

Sunderland goalkeeper Jimmy Thorpe, who played in 139 first team matches for the club and was an ever-present during the club's League Championship-winning season of 1935-36, met with his death just four days after making his final appearance. On 1 February 1936, he played at Roker Park in the 3-3 draw against Chelsea. The Sunderland 'keeper came in for some rough treatment at the hands of the Chelsea forwards and this coupled with his diabetes, resulted in his death. His Championship medal was presented to his widow.

DEBUTS

Only two Sunderland players have scored hat-tricks on their debut for the club. The first was Ronnie Turnbull who scored all four goals in a 4-1 defeat of Portsmouth at Roker Park on 29 November 1947. John Hawley achieved the feat in a 4-0 home win over Charlton Athletic on 6 October 1979.

When Derek Forster made his debut for Sunderland against Leicester City on 22 August 1964 he was aged just 15 years 184 days - thus becoming the youngest ever goalkeeper and the second youngest player to appear in the First Division.

Two Sunderland players have had unfortunate debuts. Charlie Hurley, who went on to play in 402 first team games for the Wearsiders, put through his own goals on his debut as Sunderland were beaten 7-0 by Blackpool. Scottish international John Hughes who had joined the club from Crystal Palace, made his debut against Millwall on 27 January 1973 but lasted only 15 minutes before he was forced to leave the field. It was his only appearance for the club, his injury forcing his retirement from the game.

DEFEATS - FEWEST

During the 1892-93 season, Sunderland went through the 30-match programme and suffered only four defeats as they won the First Division Championship. In recent years, the club lost six games of the 42 played in 1963-64 as they finished runners-up to Leeds United in the Second Division and were promoted to the top flight.

DEFEATS - MOST

A total of 22 defeats suffered during seasons 1956-57, 1969-70, 1984-85 and 1992-93 is the worst in the club's history. After finishing 20th in the First Division in 1956-57, the club were relegated in each of the other three seasons in which they suffered 22 defeats.

DEFEATS - WORST

Sunderland's record league defeat is 8-0, a scoreline inflicted upon the club by Sheffield Wednesday on 26 December 1911, West Ham United on 19 October 1968 and Watford on 25 September 1982. The club's worst defeat in the FA Cup came in a fourth round tie against Aston Villa when the Wearsiders lost 7-2.

DEFENSIVE RECORDS

Sunderland's best defensive record was established in 1998-99 when the club won the First Division Championship. They conceded just 28 goals in 46 matches. The club's worst defensive record was in 1957-58 when they let in 97 goals to finish 21st in the First Division and were relegated to Division Two.

DERBIES

Sunderland and Newcastle United first met in the Football League on

Christmas Eve 1898 when the Magpies won 3-2 at Roker Park with John Leslie scoring both the Wearsiders' goals. Sunderland gained revenge in the return game by winning 1-0 at St James' Park with George McLatchie the scorer. The following season Billy Hogg scored a hat-trick as Sunderland won 4-2 at St James' Park. In fact, the Wearsiders were to remain a bogey side to the Magpies, United not winning a home match against Sunderland until 1903.

On 5 December 1908, Sunderland beat Newcastle 9-1, still the biggest away victory of all time in the top flight! Yet at half-time with the scores level at 1-1 there was nothing to indicate the avalanche of goals that were to follow in the second-half. After Holley and Hogg had made it 3-1, Sunderland then netted no fewer than five goals in eight minutes before adding a ninth goal near the end. It was a remarkable result, considering that at the end of the season Newcastle were the League Champions!

During Sunderland's run to the FA Cup Final in 1912-13 they drew Newcastle United in the quarter-final. In the first game, the Magpies' playing to a tight defensive system, drew 0-0, whilst the replay at St James' Park went into extra-time after no goals had been scored in the normal 90 minutes. In extra-time, McTavish gave United the lead before Buchan and Holley put Sunderland 2-1 up. With time fast running out, Colin Veitch's shot deflected off full-back Gladwin to make the final score 2-2. The third meeting was again at St James' Park after Bob Kyle and Frank Watt had tossed a coin. With snow falling, Sunderland won 3-0 with Jackie Mordue scoring two of the goals.

Another hat-trick hero for Sunderland was Bobby Best who scored three goals in the 5-2 win over United on Christmas Day 1914.

In 1920-21, Newcastle gained their biggest victory in the meetings so far with a 6-1 win at St James' Park. When the club's met in the 1928-29 season, both sides won seven-goal thrillers. At Roker Park, Sunderland beat the Magpies 5-2 whilst in the return, United won 4-3.

Sunderland beat Newcastle 5-0 in 1930-31 but after that the games were much more even and in the four seasons from 1949-50 to 1952-53 all the four games at St James' Park ended all-square at 2-2. In 1955-56 Newcastle won 6-1 at Roker Park and then the following season put another six goals past the Wearsiders in a 6-2 home win.

Gary Rowell netted a hat-trick as Sunderland won 4-1 at St James' Park on 24 February 1979 in a Second Division encounter. The following season the two clubs met in the League Cup and after both games had ended 2-2, Sunderland won the resulting penalty shoot-out 7-6.

The clubs also met in the 1989-90 play-offs which Sunderland won 2-0 on aggregate with goals from Gates and Gabbiadini, after the first leg at Roker Park had been goalless.

When the clubs met in the Premier League in 1996-97, United won 2-1 at Sunderland, whilst the game at St James' Park ended all-square at 1-1. Sunderland's record against Newcastle United is:

	P	W	D	L	F	A
Premier League	2	0	1	1	2	3
Division One	100	34	27	39	159	162
Division Two	14	4	7	3	17	13
Play-Offs	2	1	1	0	2	0
FA Cup	8	3	3	2	11	8
Football League Cup	2	0	2	0	4	4
TOTAL	128	42	41	45	195	190

DISMISSALS

The first Sunderland player to receive his marching orders in a Football League game was Hughie Wilson when he was sent-off in the 5-0 defeat at Stoke on 14 March 1896.

When the Wearsiders played Leeds United in the fifth round of the 1966-67 FA Cup competition, the first two matches were drawn, necessitating a third meeting at Hull City's Boothferry Park. With the score at 1-1, the Yorkshire club were awarded a hotly disputed penalty after Irwin had allegedly tripped Jimmy Greenhoff in the box. Protests from the Sunderland players led to both George Herd and George Mulhall being dismissed. Sunderland finished the game with nine men and went out of the competition 2-1 after Johnny Giles had converted the spot-kick.

In the Premier League game against Arsenal at Highbury on 26 September 1996, Sunderland had three sent-off. Manager Peter Reid was shown the red card following the dismissals of Scott and Stewart, the latter later had his red card rescinded.

DOCHERTY, MICK

The son of Tommy Docherty, he was sent by his father to Burnley where the much-travelled manager believed he would receive the best preparation for professional football. At Turf Moor, Mick Docherty soon showed his leadership qualities, captaining the Clarets to FA Youth Cup success in 1968. After captaining the club's Central League side, he made his first team debut in the First Division as an 18-year-old in a 1-1 home draw against Stoke City. He soon became an established first team player and over the next four seasons was a virtual ever-present. In April 1973 in a match against Huddersfield Town, he tore knee ligaments and though he had recovered for the start of the following season, he was injured again in the opening game of that campaign. He played in just one more game for Burnley over the next two years before being released.

After a short spell at Manchester City, he was transferred to Sunderland where former Burnley player and manager Jimmy Adamson was in charge. He made his debut in a 1-0 home defeat by Coventry City in January 1977 and though the club was relegated at the end of that campaign, Docherty had turned in a number of impressive performances. Later appointed club captain, he scored his first-ever league goal in Sunderland's 1-1 draw at Blackpool in March 1978. He had played in 81 first team games for the Wearsiders when he retired and joined the Roker Park coaching staff.

When Ken Knighton was relieved of his duties in April 1981, Docherty took temporary charge and he faced the difficult task of beating Liverpool at Anfield in the final match of the season to secure the Wearsiders' First Division status. Remarkably, a Stan Cummins goal gave the club a 1-0 win.

His first permanent managerial appointment came at Hartlepool in 1983 from where he became his father's assistant at Wolves. He later returned to Burnley as assistant-manager to Frank Casper before holding a similar position at Hull City. He joined Rochdale as coach in 1991 before taking over as manager in 1994, a position he held for two years.

DOIG, NED

Born in Forfar in October 1866, goalkeeper Ned Doig began his career with Arbroath in 1883. He then signed for Blackburn Rovers but made only one appearance before joining Sunderland where he came under the careful guidance of manager Tom Watson.

He made his Football League debut for Sunderland in a 4-0 win at West Bromwich Albion on 20 September 1890, but despite keeping a clean sheet in what was the club's first success, he had not been registered and so the Wearsiders were fined £50 and had their first two points deducted!

The first in a long line of notable Sunderland 'keepers, Ned Doig was ever-present in seven seasons and helped the club win four League Championships in his 14 years at Roker Park. He won five full caps for Scotland, the first against Northern Ireland in 1887 when he was with Arbroath. His three appearances at full international level whilst he was with Sunderland were all against England, his first resulting in a 2-1 win for Scotland.

After appearing in 456 first team games for Sunderland, Doig joined his former manager Tom Watson, by then with Liverpool, in 1904. He remained at Anfield until 1908, making 51 appearances. He played eight games during Liverpool's championship-winning season of 1905-06 and had been ever-present the previous season as Liverpool clinched the Second Division title conceding just 25 goals. He eventually retired in 1908, handing over to another fine goalkeeper Sam Hardy.

DRAWS
Sunderland played their greatest number of drawn league matches in a single season in 1954-55 and 1994-95, when 18 of their matches ended all square and their fewest in 1908-09, when only two of their 38 matches were drawn. The club's highest scoring draw is 5-5, at home to Liverpool in 1906-07 and away at Middlesbrough in 1936-37.

DUNS, LEN
Outside-right Len Duns joined the Wearsiders from Newcastle West End in September 1933 and worked his way through the ranks before making his first team debut in a 2-2 draw at Portsmouth on 2 November 1935. The following week he made his home debut and scored two goals in a 4-2 win over Preston North End.

His best season for the club in terms of goals scored was 1936-37 when he netted 21 in 45 League and Cup outings. Included in this total were five FA Cup goals in successive ties as the Wearsiders won the way through to the final where they beat Preston North End 3-1.

During the war years, he appeared in 25 games and when the Football League resumed in 1946-47, he was still a regular member of the club's first team. He went on to score 54 goals in 247 League and Cup games for Sunderland, playing his last game against Preston North End on 22 March 1952.

DURBAN, ALAN
A skilful midfield player, Alan Durban began his Football League career with Cardiff City and made his first team debut against Derby County, the club with which he was to make his name, in September 1959. After 52 league outings for the Bluebirds, Tim Ward the Derby County manager paid £10,000 for his services in July 1963.

Durban had two distinct phases at the Baseball Ground, the first as a goalscoring inside-forward and the second as an intelligent midfield player. In 1964-65 he scored 24 goals and went on to score 112 goals in 403 games for County including four hat-tricks. However, his best days for Derby were in midfield. His greatest attribute was his ability to find space in a crowded penalty area, arriving late to score a large percentage of his goals from close range.

He had won 27 Welsh caps by the time he left Derby to join Shrewsbury Town, where he became player-manager. After steering them out of the Fourth Division in 1974-75 and later into the Second Division, he left Gay Meadow to manage Stoke City. He took the Potters into the First Division before joining Sunderland in the summer of 1981 after he had received a more tempting offer.

After three troubled years at Sunderland in which the club always struggled in the relegation zone of the First Division, he was sacked and six months later returned to manage his first club Cardiff City. It was a bad move with the Ninian Park club plummeting from the Second to the Fourth Division. In 1986 he left the club to run an indoor tennis club in Telford.

Sunderland's full league record under Alan Durban is:

P	W	D	L	F	A
112	31	34	47	114	158

DURHAM CHALLENGE CUP
Formerly known as the Northumberland and Durham Challenge Cup, it was first contested for in 1883-84 when Sunderland were the winners of this newly named competition. Sunderland beat Miltswell Burn 7-0, Jarrow 5-2 and Hamsterley Rangers 3-1 to reach the semi-final. After a goalless draw with Hobson Wanderers, Sunderland won the replay 6-0 to reach the first-ever final of the Durham Challenge Cup. Though the Wearsiders beat Darlington 4-3, officials from the Feethams club objected to the intimidation shown by several Sunderland players. The game had to be replayed but the Wearsiders still triumphed 2-0 with goals from McDonald and Joyce.

In 1884-85, Sunderland beat Castletown 23-0 in what was supposedly a first round tie but as their opponents only had eight men (though Sunderland did lend them three players) it was changed to a friendly. Other victories followed against Wearmouth and Birtley to put Sunderland into their second final where their opponents were once again Darlington. This time Darlington won 3-0.

The club didn't enter the competition in 1885-86 deciding to concentrate on the English Cup but returned the following season to reach their third successive final after beating Birtley 2-0, Gateshead 3-2 and Whitburn 5-3. Yet again Darlington were the club's opponents in the final - the only goal of the game by Davison giving Sunderland the cup.

In 1887-88, Sunderland beat Durham University 8-0, Whitburn 1-0, Southwick 7-1 and Darlington 2-1 after the first game had been drawn 1-1. In the final, Sunderland defeated Bishop Auckland 2-1 to win the trophy for a third time.

After being drawn against Sunderland Albion in both the English Cup and Durham Challenge Cup, the club decided to withdraw from both competitions but in 1889-90, they re-entered and beat Birtley 4-0 and Darlington St Augustine's 1-0 to reach the final where Darlington again provided the opposition. Sunderland were the victors, winning a hard fought game to 2-0 to become cup holders for a fourth time in five attempts.

E

EARLY GROUNDS

The club's first regular playing area was the Blue House Field at Hendon which was situated next to the original Blue House pub and is now Commercial Road, Hendon. The club which had been formed in 1879 was having difficulty in meeting the annual rent of £10 and so in 1882 moved to their second ground at Groves Field, Ashbrooke. Close to what is now the Ashbrooke Sports Club, only four home matches were ever played there, the club preferring to play away games.

A year later, the club moved north of the Wear to Horatio Street, Roker, where on one side of the pitch there was a claypit and brickworks, the ground often being referred to as a 'Clay Dolly' field.

In September 1884, Sunderland rented their first enclosed ground at Abbs Field, Fulwell. At first the rent was quite reasonable but as the gates increased, so did the ground rent, and in March 1886 the club moved to a ground on Newcastle Road which was owned by the Thompson sisters.

Prior to the club's first game at the ground on 3 April 1886 against Darlington, a 1,000 seater stand was built by club supporters. Within 12 months of their move, the crowds had swelled from 1,000 to 8,000 but in 1888 the club were expelled from the FA Cup and Jimmy Allan and a group of other players broke away to form Sunderland Albion.

Just as it seemed that they would become the number one outfit in the town, Sunderland appointed Tom Watson as manager and, backed by Richard Thompson, he assembled a team which gained the club membership of the Football League in 1890.

The ground at Newcastle Road flourished, a new stand was built and in March 1891, was the venue for an England v Wales international. As the crowds increased the club had to seek a new ground, for not only had the ground rent risen to £100 per annum but they had also failed to buy the freehold. The club's final game at Newcastle Road was on 23 April 1898 when they beat Nottingham Forest 4-0, after which they moved to Roker Park.

ELECTION TO THE FOOTBALL LEAGUE

At the AGM of the Football League on 2 May 1890, Sunderland were one of eight clubs - the others being Burnley, Notts County and Stoke (who were all seeking re-election) and Darwen, Grimsby Town, Newton Heath and Sunderland Albion, all trying to win one of the three available places.

The Revd Hindle and Mr Marr were sent to the meeting on Sunderland's behalf and put forward a very convincing case. They stated that if Sunderland were to be elected they would need to make eleven lengthy journeys during the season compared to their opponents' one and that the club's playing record was much better than some teams already in the League. They also stated that they would be prepared to help visiting clubs with expenses. Not surprisingly, the club were admitted to the Football League for the 1890-91 season along with Burnley and Notts County.

ELLIOTT, BILLY

Billy Elliott was spotted playing football in his home town by Bradford Park Avenue during the Second World War and after joining them as an amateur, signed professional forms in March 1942. After scoring 21 goals in 176 games for the Yorkshire club he became Burnley's record signing when he joined the Turf Moor club in the summer of 1951 for a fee of £25,000.

Billy Elliott immediately became a regular in Burnley's First Division side and such was his impact during his first season in the top flight that he was chosen to go on England's European Tour in May 1952, winning his first full cap in a 1-1 draw with Italy in Florence. He was probably at the peak of his career the following season, appearing in three more international, scoring three goals and representing the Football League on three occasions. His last game for the Clarets was in a 5-1 destruction of Sunderland and just two months later in June 1953, he was on his way to Roker Park for a record £26,000 to become part of the then most expensive club side ever assembled in England.

He made his debut for the Wearsiders in a 5-3 defeat at Charlton Athletic on the opening day of the 1953-54 campaign and over the next five seasons, scored 26 goals in 212 League and Cup appearances. Elliott played in just one more representative game during his Sunderland days, scoring in a 4-2 win for the Football League against the Irish League at Anfield. However, success at club level was a little harder to come by, though Sunderland finished fourth in the First Division in 1955 and reached the semi-finals of the FA Cup in 1955 and 1956. Following the club's relegation in 1957-58, Elliott spent a year in the Second Division at Roker Park, his last season in league football.

After a spell with non-League Wisbech Town, he flew out to Tripoli to become the national coach to the Libyan FA before holding a variety of coaching and managerial appointments.

After an earlier five year spell as trainer-coach at Roker Park, he returned from Norway in 1978 to replace the departed Jimmy Adamson as Sunderland's caretaker manager. Despite steering the Wearsiders to within one point of promotion to the First Division in 1979 it wasn't enough to secure him the job on a permanent basis and he left to spend four years as manager of Darlington.

Sunderland's full league record under Billy Elliott is:

P	W	D	L	F	A
27	13	8	6	46	29

ELLIOTT, SHAUN

An England 'B' international, Shaun Elliott joined the Wearsiders from his home-town club Haydon Bridge in January 1975 and made his first team debut in the First Division match against Leicester City at Filbert Street two years later, a game in which the Foxes won 2-0. He missed the next match against Stoke City but then played in the remaining 18 games of the season. Over the next nine seasons, the popular defender missed very few matches and was an important member of the side that regained its place in the top flight in 1979-80. Though he never scored for the Wearsiders in either of the cup competitions, he netted 11 league goals including four in that promotion-winning campaign, two of them in the 5-0 defeat of Watford. He had appeared in 368 first team games for the club when in August 1986 he was transferred to Norwich City for £140,000.

Hampered by injuries during his stay at Carrow Road, he jumped at the chance to join Blackpool two years later and appeared in 80 League and Cup games for the Seasiders before entering non-League football with Whitley Bay and later Durham City.

Shaun Elliott

ELLIS, BILLY
Wolverhampton-born winger Billy Ellis joined Sunderland from Bilston Juniors in 1919 but had to wait until March 1920 before making his debut in a 2-0 win at Middlesbrough. After establishing himself as a first team regular midway through the 1921-22 season, he helped the club finish the following season as runners-up to Liverpool in the First

Division championship. Though never a prolific goalscorer, he had found the net six times in the first 11 games of the 1925-26 season before a knee injury hampered his progress. He returned to full fitness the following season and had scored 31 goals in 202 games when the Sunderland board allowed him to leave Roker Park in November 1927 and join Birmingham.

He scored eight goals in 32 games for the St Andrews club before leaving to play for Lincoln City where he ended his league career.

ENGLAND, ERNIE
Left-back Ernie England joined Sunderland from Derby County where he had appeared in the club's youth team. The tough-tackling defender made his debut for the Wearsiders in a 1-0 defeat at Manchester City on 27 December 1919. After appearing in just seven league games during that 1919-20 season, England established himself in the early part of the following campaign and held his place for ten seasons. He was ever-present in 1922-23 when the Wearsiders were runners-up to Liverpool, six points behind the Anfield club.

England went on to play in 351 League and Cup games for Sunderland before leaving Roker Park in October 1930 to join West Ham United. One of his first games for the Hammers was against Sunderland at Upton Park in a fixture that ended all-square at 1-1.

EUROPEAN CUP WINNERS CUP
Sunderland's 1-0 FA Cup Final victory over Leeds United in 1973 led to the club's only ever appearance in a European competition in 1973-74.

In the first round of the European Cup Winners' Cup, Sunderland were drawn against Hungarian side Vasas Budapest. The first leg in Hungary saw Billy Hughes open the scoring before a late Dennis Tueart goal gave the Wearsiders a 2-0 victory. The second leg at Roker Park only attracted a crowd of 22,762 which was well below the club's average gate at the time. This was probably due to the fact that Sunderland increased admission prices for the game. In a hard fought match, a Dennis Tueart penalty separated the sides to give the Wearsiders a 3-0 aggregate win.

In the second round, Sporting Lisbon of Portugal visited Roker Park. The Wearsiders took the lead after 33 minutes when Lisbon goalkeeper Damas was adjudged to have carried the ball over his own goal-line when collecting a cross from Bobby Kerr. The home side extended their lead on the hour-mark when Horswill headed home another Kerr cross. Rather than settle for a 2-0 win, the Wearsiders went in search of a third goal but this left them exposed at the back and with just five minutes to go, Lisbon centre-forward Yazalde headed home Chico's cross.

In the second leg, Sunderland attempted to adopt a defensive approach but went a goal down after a dreadful clearance by Jim Montgomery. The ball fell at the feet of Nelson who played in Yazalde to level the tie on aggregate. Following David Young's obstruction on a Lisbon forward, the home side were awarded a free-kick in the penalty area which was eventually scrambled home by Fraguite. Though Dennis Tueart later hit a post, there was no further scoring and the Portuguese went through to the third round 3-2 on aggregate.

EVER-PRESENTS
There have been 57 Sunderland players who have been ever-present throughout a league season. The greatest number of ever-present seasons by a Sunderland player is seven by Ned Doig. Next in line is fellow goal-keeper Jim Montgomery with five.

F

FA CUP

Sunderland entered the FA Cup (although it was then known as the English Cup) for the first time in 1884-85 but lost 3-1 at Redcar. It was 1890-91 before the club made any impact on the competition, beating Everton 1-0, league leaders Darwen 2-0 and Nottingham Forest 4-0. The Wearsiders reached the semi-finals but lost 2-0 to Notts County after the first game had ended 3-3. The club reached the semi-final stage again the following season. After gaining revenge over Notts County whom they beat 4-0, the north-east club defeated Accrington 3-1 and Stoke 4-0 after a 2-2 draw at Roker Park but were beaten 4-1 by Aston Villa in the semi-final at Bramall Lane. The club reached their third FA Cup semi-final in 1894-95 after beating Fairfield 11-1, their biggest ever victory in the competition, they defeated Lancashire clubs Preston North End 2-0 and Bolton Wanderers 2-1 before losing to Aston Villa.

The Wearsiders reached their first FA Cup Final in 1912-13. They beat Clapton Orient 6-0, Manchester City 2-0 (after the first meeting between the clubs had been abandoned due to a pitch invasion) Swindon Town 4-2 and Newcastle United 3-2 (after the first game had been goalless). In the final Sunderland played Aston Villa who had beaten the Wearsiders on each of the four previous occasions they had met in the FA Cup. Despite hitting the woodwork twice, Sunderland went down 1-0 to a Tom Barber goal.

In 1913-14 Sunderland recorded another big victory when they beat non-League Chatham 9-0 with former Huddersfield Town player Jimmy Richardson netting four of the goals.

In the first round tie against Hull City in 1919-20, Charlie Buchan also found the net four times as the Tigers were beaten 6-2. The club chalked up another big win against non-League opposition when they beat Boston 8-1 with both Kelly and Halliday scoring hat-tricks.

The club reached the semi-final stage again in 1930-31. After beating Southampton (2-0) Bolton Wanderers (3-1 after a 1-1 draw) Sheffield

Sunderland's FA Cup winning side of 1973
Back row left to right: D. Young, V. Halom, D. Watson, J. Montgomery, D. Malone, R.Pitt
Front row left to right: M. Horsewell, B. Kerr, D. Tueart, B. Hughes, I. Porterfield, R. Guthrie

United (2-1) and Exeter City (4-2 after a 1-1 draw) they met Birmingham at Elland Road. Despite a lot of pressure it was the Midlands club that went through to the final, winning 2-0.

After the Wearsiders had drawn 4-4 at Derby County in the sixth round of the 1932-33 competition, they lost the replay at home to the Rams 1-0 in front of what was Roker Park's record attendance of 75,118.

The following season, the club suffered their heaviest FA Cup defeat, losing 7-2 at Aston Villa. In 1934-35 Sunderland played in what was probably the finest game of football ever seen at Goodison Park. After a 1-1 draw at Roker Park, the replay produced ten goals with Everton winning 6-4.

The club reached their second final in 1936-37 after beating Southampton at The Dell 3-2, Luton Town 3-1 after a 2-2 draw, Swansea Town 3-0, Wolves 4-0 after the first two games had been drawn and Millwall 2-1 in the semi-final. In the final, Sunderland found themselves a goal down to Preston North End but second-half goals from Gurney, Carter and Burbanks gave the Wearsiders a 3-1 victory and the FA Cup for the first time in their history.

The following season, Sunderland were knocked out at the semi-final stage by Huddersfield Town 3-1 as they tried to retain the trophy they had won in 1936-37.

The club then reached the semi-finals of the FA Cup in two successive seasons in the mid-fifties. In 1954-55 Sunderland beat Burnley 1-0, Preston North End 2-0 after a 3-3 draw, Swansea Town 1-0 after a 2-2 draw and Wolves 2-0 before losing 1-0 to Manchester City at a very wet Villa Park. In 1955-56 the Wearsiders beat Norwich City 4-2, York City 2-1 after a goalless draw. Sheffield United 1-0 after another goalless draw and rivals Newcastle United 2-0, but were well beaten 3-0 in the semi-final by Birmingham City.

In 1972-73 Sunderland reached their third FA Cup Final after beating Notts County 2-0 after a 1-1 draw, Reading 3-1 after a 1-1 draw, Manchester City 3-1 after a 2-2 draw, Luton Town 2-0 and Arsenal 2-1 in the semi-final at Hillsborough. In the final, an Ian Porterfield goal and some magnificent saves by Jim Montgomery led to the Wearsiders, who were then a Second Division club, beating the mighty Leeds United 1-0.

Sunderland last reached the FA Cup Final in 1991-92, beating Port Vale 3-0, Oxford United 3-2, West Ham United 3-2 after a 1-1 draw, Chelsea 2-1 after a 1-1 draw and Norwich City in the semi-final 1-0. In the final, the Wearsiders harried their opponents Liverpool and as half-time arrived, deserved to be level. Goals by Thomas and Rush ended any hopes Sunderland had of lifting the cup. Somebody though, forgot to put the medals in the right order. So when a dejected Sunderland team trooped up the steps they were presented with the winners medals and had to swap them afterwards with Liverpool, who were given the losers medals.

FA CUP FINALS
Sunderland have appeared in four FA Cup Finals, winning the trophy on two occasions:

1913	v Aston Villa (at Crystal Palace)	0-1
1937	v Preston North End (at Wembley)	3-1
1973	v Leeds United (at Wembley)	1-0
1992	v Liverpool (at Wembley)	0-2

FA CUP SEMI-FINALS
Sunderland have participated in 11 FA Cup semi-finals up to the end of the 1998-99 season.

FANZINES
There are a number of Sunderland fanzines. They include 'A Love Supreme', 'Sex and Chocolate', 'The Sunderland Fanatic', 'The Black Cat' and 'It's the hope I can't stand'.

FARQUHAR, BILLY
Billy Farquhar joined Sunderland from Elgin City in January 1899 and made his first team debut in a 1-0 win at Sheffield Wednesday the following month. He ended that season with four goals in 10 games and in 1899-1900 had his best campaign in terms of goals scored when he found the net six times in 19 outings.

Moving from his usual inside-forward position to wing-half, Farquhar's strong tackling and good distributional skills were a great asset to the club's cause. Though he won a League Championship medal in 1901-02 it was the following season before he established himself as a first team regular when, like Ned Doig, he missed just one game.

He went on to appear in 195 League and Cup games spread over nine seasons before hanging up his boots.

FERGUSON, MATTHEW
Wing-half Matthew Ferguson joined the club from Mossend Brigade in the summer of 1896 and went straight into the Sunderland side for the opening game of the 1896-97 season, a 1-0 defeat at home to Bury. That season, Ferguson's first with the club, he was ever-present and was one of the club's best players when they beat Newton Heath 2-0 in the last Test Match to secure their First Division status.

Over the next six seasons, Ferguson was a virtual ever-present in the Sunderland side and in 1901-02 turned in a number of outstanding performances as the club won the League Championship, finishing three points ahead of runners-up Everton.

He had played in 182 League and Cup games for the club up to the end of the 1901-02 season when in June 1902 he died at the tragically young age of 29.

FINANCIAL CRISIS

In 1881, two years after Sunderland had been formed, they suffered a financial crisis which was saved by one of their members auctioning one of his prize canary pets. The bird and cage was raffled and fetched £1 which was enough to see them out of immediate fiscal embarrassment!

FIRST DIVISION

Sunderland have had seven spells in the First Division. Elected to the Football League in 1890, the club's first spell lasted until 1958 - the last club able to claim the distinction of playing in only the First Division. During this time they won the League Championship on six occasions - 1891-92, 1892-93, 1894-95, 1901-02, 1912-13 and 1935-36 and were runners-up on five occasions. After being relegated in 1957-58 the club spent six seasons in the Second Division before returning to the top flight at the end of the 1963-64 season.

After six seasons of struggle in which their highest position was 15th, the Wearsiders were relegated in 1969-70 and did not return to the First Division until 1976-77. In a season in which the club had three managers - Stokoe, McFarlane and Adamson, they ended the campaign in 20th place and lost their First Division status after just one season.

It was 1980-81 before the Wearsiders played First Division football again, their fourth spell lasting five seasons before they were relegated at the end of a season in which they had reached the League Cup Final. Following four seasons in the Second Division and one in the Third Division, Sunderland returned to the top flight for a fifth spell but again it lasted just one season.

Following reorganisation in 1992, Sunderland found themselves playing First Division football again but won promotion to the Premier League in 1995-96. However, after just one season the club returned to the First Division and in 1997-98 reached the play-off final against Charlton Athletic at Wembley but after a 4-4 draw, lost 7-6 on penalties.

In 1998-99 the Wearsiders ran away with the First Division Championship, finishing 18 points clear of runners-up Bradford City, and scoring 105 goals in the process.

FIRST LEAGUE MATCH
Sunderland played their first Football League match on 13 September 1890 when their opponents at Newcastle Road were Burnley. The Turf Moor club were one of the re-elected sides from the previous season and it was expected that Sunderland would easily account for the Lancashire club. Despite two goals from Spence, who thus had the honour of scoring the club's first league goal, Burnley won 3-2. The Sunderland team for their first league match was: W.Kirkley; T.Porteous; J.Oliver; H.Wilson; J.Auld; W.Gibson; J.Spence; J.Millar; J.Campbell; J.Scott and D.Hannah.

FIRST MATCH
The club played its first competitive game on 13 November 1880 against Ferryhill at the Blue House Field, losing 1-0. Newspaper reports of the day indicate that five of the club's best players were absent but that doesn't alter the result!

FLEMING, CHARLIE
Scottish international forward Charlie Fleming who scored twice against Northern Ireland on his only international appearance joined Sunderland from East Fife in January 1955 for a fee of £7,000 plus Tommy Wright who moved to the Bayview Park club after scoring 55 goals in 180 games for the Wearsiders.

Charlie Fleming who had scored 164 goals for East Fife and won two League Cup winners' medals, made his Sunderland debut in a goalless draw at Blackpool on 5 February 1955 but soon gave an indication of what the future held when he netted eight goals in 17 League and Cup games towards the end of that season.

In 1955-56, Fleming was the club's top scorer with 32 League and Cup goals in 46 games including hat-tricks against Portsmouth (Home 4-2) and Norwich City (Home 4-2), the Canaries being defeated in the third round of the FA Cup. The Dunfermline-born striker didn't always have his shooting boots on because one of his efforts in the Aston Villa game went wide of the upright and removed a nearby policeman's helmet! The following season he continued to find the net with great regularity with 27 goals in 42 games but

65

after scoring 71 goals in 122 League and Cup appearances, he was rather surprisingly allowed to leave Roker Park and join non-League Bath City as player-manager. He later held a similar post with Trowbridge Town.

FLOODLIGHTS
Sunderland played their first game under floodlights on 10 May 1933 when they won 3-0 against Racing Club De Paris in Paris.

In December 1952, Roker Park became only the second top flight club to have floodlighting installed. The lights were first switched on for a friendly match against Dundee on 11 December 1952, a game which Sunderland won 5-3. On 14 November 1955 the famous Russian side Moscow Dynamo played under the Roker floodlights and beat Sunderland 1-0 in front of an all-ticket crowd of 55,000.

In 1973 the floodlights were replaced for the European Cup Winners' Cup competition at a cost of £22,000.

FOGARTY, AMBROSE
Signed from Irish League club Glentoran for a fee of £4,500 in October 1957, Ambrose Fogarty played his first game for the Wearsiders in a 3-2 win at Birmingham City the following month. Following the club's relegation at the end of the 1957-58 season, Fogarty suffered a series of niggling injuries and made only three appearances in the club's first-ever Second Division campaign.

He returned to full fitness the following season which was his most successful in terms of goals scored, 12 in 37 appearances including a spell of 10 in 12 games midway through the campaign. His form that season led to him winning the first of 11 international caps for the Republic of Ireland when he played against West Germany. A regular member of the Sunderland side for the next three seasons, he scored his only hat-trick for the club on 9 December 1961 when Swansea Town were beaten 7-2.

Fogarty went on to score 44 goals in 174 League and Cup games before joining Hartlepool United for a fee of £10,000 in November 1963. He spent four seasons at the Victoria Ground, scoring 22 goals in 128 league games.

FOOTBALL LEAGUE CUP
With the exception of 1984-85 and 1998-99, Sunderland have failed to make much impact upon the League (later Milk, Littlewoods, Rumbelows, Coca Cola and Worthington) Cup.

The club's first-ever match in the competition on 26 October 1960 saw them lose 4-3 at Brentford after they had been 3-1 up at half-time. However, in 1961-62, the club reached the fifth round after beating Bolton Wanderers 1-0 after a 1-1 draw, winning 5-2 against Walsall with Brian Clough scoring a hat-trick and Hull City 2-1 and receiving a bye in the fourth round. In the quarter-final tie, the Wearsiders lost 4-1 at home to Norwich City.

The following season, the club went a stage further and reached the semi-finals. In the second round, Oldham Athletic were beaten 7-1 with Kiernan, Clough and Fogarty scoring two goals apiece. There then followed victories over Scunthorpe United 2-0, Portsmouth 2-1 after a goalless draw and Blackburn Rovers 3-2. In the two-leg semi-final, Sunderland met Aston Villa but the tie was as good as over after the first leg as the Wearsiders went down 3-1 at Roker Park. They battled hard for a goalless draw at Villa Park but failed to make the Cup Final. In 1979-80, Sunderland beat Newcastle United 7-6 on a penalty shoot-out after both matches had ended all-square at 2-2 and Manchester City 1-0 after a 1-1 draw at Maine Road. The fourth round match also went to two games but after being held to a 1-1 draw at home to West Ham United, Sunderland lost the replay at Upton Park 2-1.

In 1984-85, the Wearsiders reached the League Cup Final for the first time in their history. Crystal Palace were beaten 2-1 on aggregate and Nottingham Forest 1-0 after extra-time in the second meeting between the clubs after the first had been draw 1-1. The club's fourth round meeting against Tottenham Hotspur also went to two games, for after a goalless draw at Roker Park, goals from Chisholm and Walker gave Sunderland a surprise 2-1 win at White Hart Lane. Clive Walker was on target again in the fifth round as the Wearsiders beat Watford at Vicarage Road 1-0. Two goals from Colin West gave Sunderland victory 2-0 in the first leg against Chelsea in front of a Roker Park crowd of 32,440. In the return at Stamford Bridge, two goals from Walker and a superb strike by West gave Sunderland a 3-2 win and an aggregate victory of 5-2. In the final, Sunderland met Norwich City who had knocked the Wearsiders out of the cup in the last two seasons. The game was not a classic and was settled by an Asa Hartford shot that took a deflection off Chisholm to take the cup to Carrow Road, although it could have been a different story if Clive Walker hadn't missed a second-half penalty for Sunderland.

Sunderland's best performance in the League Cup in recent years was in 1998-99 when the club reached the semi-final stage only to lose over two legs to Leicester City.

FORD, TREVOR

Welsh international Trevor Ford chose to start his league career with his home-town club of Swansea in 1944, despite a number of other clubs wanting to sign him. After scoring 44 goals in 41 games for the Swans in the 1945-46 season and nine in the opening six games of the following campaign, Ford left the Vetch Field to join Aston Villa for a fee of £10,000. He made his Villa debut in a 2-0 win at Highbury in January 1947 and in nine games that season, scored nine goals. In terms of goals scored, his best seasons were 1947-48 and 1949-50 when he netted 18 in each campaign although on 27 December 1948, he scored four goals as Villa beat Wolves 5-1. In October 1950, Ford left Villa Park after scoring 61 goals in 128 games and signed for Sunderland for £30,000.

After playing his first game in Sunderland colours in a 3-0 defeat at Chelsea, he scored a hat-trick on his home debut when Sheffield Wednesday were beaten 5-1. He top scored for the club over the next two seasons, netting a hat-trick in a 4-1 home win over Chelsea in February 1952 and four goals in a 5-2 defeat of Manchester City at Maine Road in November 1952. He netted another hat-trick at the start of the 1953-54 campaign when Arsenal were beaten 4-1 but a few weeks later, after scoring 70 goals in 117 League and Cup games, he joined Cardiff City for what was then the Welsh club's record fee of £30,000.

Though not as prolific a scorer as in his early days in the game, he did net four goals in two Welsh Cup games when Pembroke Borough were beaten 7-0 in 1954-55 and 9-0 in 1955-56. He had scored 59 goals in 119 outings when he fell out with Cardiff manager Trevor Morris, following his decision to play him at outside-right.

After leaving Ninian Park, Ford was banned *sine die* by the Football League following his revelations about the Wearsiders in his autobiography 'I lead the attack'. Between 1957 and 1960, he played in Holland with PSV Eindhoven. After a brief spell with Newport County, Ford ended his playing career with non-League Romford.

FOUNDATION

Sunderland were founded in 1879 as the Sunderland and District Teachers' Association Football Club by Scottish schoolmaster James Allen who was working at Hendon Boarding School, at a meeting in the Adults School, Norfolk Street. Due to financial difficulties, the team soon opened its ranks to players outside the teaching profession and in October 1880 became Sunderland AFC.

FREIGHT ROVER TROPHY

A competition designed solely and specifically for Associate Members of the Football League, the Freight Rover Trophy replaced the initial Associate Members Cup for the 1984-85 season.

Following their relegation to the Third Division after the play-offs, Sunderland's only season in the competition was 1987-88. A 3-0 win at Scarborough in the preliminary round took the Wearsiders into the first round where they were drawn at home against Rotherham United. A crowd of only 6,750 witnessed a superb display of attacking football from the home side who ran out winners 7-1 with goals from Bertschin (2) Burley Corner, Owers, Lemon and Moore. Another home tie in round two saw a Marco Gabbiadini goal give Sunderland a 1-0 victory over Crewe Alexandra. The third round draw again favoured the Wearsiders with home advantage but despite having most of the play, they went out of the competition, 1-0 to Hartlepool United.

FULL MEMBERS' CUP

The competition was the idea of Ron Noades, the then Crystal Palace chairman, following the European ban on English clubs.

Sunderland first entered the competition in its inaugural season of 1985-86 where their opponents in the first round were Grimsby Town. After losing the first leg at Blundell Park 3-2 in front of just 2,435 spectators, goals from Gates and Hodgson gave the Wearsiders a 2-1 home win and took the tie to a penalty shoot-out. The two goalscorers along with Alan Kennedy were successful from the spot and took Sunderland through to a quarter-final meeting with Manchester City at Maine Road. The game was goalless and went to another penalty shoot-out which the home side won 4-3.

A penalty shoot-out also decided the club's first game in the 1986-87 competition against Barnsley at Roker Park. After a 1-1 draw, the Wearsiders beat their Yorkshire rivals 8-7 to progress to a second round meeting with Bradford City at Bradford Northern's Odsal Stadium. Despite goals from Armstrong and Lemon, Sunderland lost 3-2.

G

GABBIADINI, MARCO

Capped by England at Under-21 and 'B' international level, Nottingham-born striker Marco Gabbiadini began his Football League career with York City where he scored 18 goals in 71 games before following his manager Denis Smith to Sunderland for a fee of £80,000 in September 1987.

After making his debut for the Wearsiders in a 2-0 home defeat by Chester City, he scored two goals in each of his next three league games for Sunderland and as the club won the Third Division Championship that season, Gabbiadini was the top scorer with 21 goals. Gabbiadini was also the leading scorer the following season and netted his first hat-trick for the club in a 4-0 home win over Ipswich Town. In 1989 he struck another hat-trick in a 4-0 defeat of Watford and after the club had finished sixth to win a place in the play-offs, he scored in the semi-final second leg win over Newcastle United at St James' Park. After surprisingly gaining promotion to the top flight at the expense of Swindon Town who won the play-off final but were later relegated because of financial irregularities, the Wearsiders could only manage 38 league goals in Division One and were relegated - Gabbiadini scoring nine. After having topped the club's scoring lists for four successive seasons, Gabbiadini, who had scored 87 goals in 185 games including a hat-trick against Charlton Athletic in his penultimate game for the club, departed to Crystal Palace for a club record fee of £1.5 million.

Unable to settle at Selhurst Park, he moved to Derby County for £1 million just three months after joining the London club.

The bustling centre-forward soon became a great favourite with the Rams' fans and in five years at the Baseball Ground scored 68 goals in 227 games before losing his first team place. He had loan spells at Birmingham City and Oxford United before joining Stoke City on a free transfer after a period playing abroad with Greek side Panionios. He later returned to Bootham Crescent to end his league career with his first club.

GALLACHER, PATSY

A Roker regular for 307 League and Cup games, Patsy Gallacher showed great promise as a Linwood schoolboy footballer and played for a local church side, Linwood St Connel's before joining his home-town club, Bridge of Weir FC. In 1927 he moved south to join Sunderland's ground staff, turning professional in September 1928.

One of new manager Johnny Cochrane's first signings, Gallacher made his First Division debut as a left-winger in a 1-0 home defeat by Arsenal on 21 September 1929. He was recalled to the side at inside-left just before Christmas and struck up a good understanding with centre-forward Bob Gurney. After Raich Carter joined the club, Gallacher switched to inside-right and the three players became the most effective partnership in League football in the 1930s.

Gallacher was a fine dribbler with good ball control and a natural body swerve. Though he was primarily a provider, his own strike-rate improved as his career with the Wearsiders wore on.

He netted the first of six hat-tricks for the club in a 3-1 win at Blackburn Rovers in 1932-33 and two the following season as Liverpool were beaten 4-1 and Middlesbrough 4-0 at Ayresome Park. In 1934-35 he scored 20 league goals in 35 games including another hat-trick in a 4-0 defeat of Chelsea. Sunderland's Championship-winning season of 1935-36 was his best. Although he scored 19 goals in 37 league games including three in a 7-2 win over Blackburn Rovers, his was essentially a supporting role to Carter and Gurney, who scored 31 goals apiece. Between them the three players accounted for 81 of the club's 109 goals in that memorable campaign. His last hat-trick for the club came in March 1937 as Wolverhampton Wanderers were beaten 6-2.

That season of 1936-37 saw Sunderland lift the FA Cup and Gallacher was ever-present in the nine-match run. He only scored twice but they were vital goals. He scored the winner at The Dell where the Wearsiders beat Southampton 3-2 and then one in the semi-final win over Millwall.

His only international cap for Scotland came in a 2-1 defeat against

Northern Ireland in Belfast in October 1934 and although he scored, he never won another international honour. He began the 1938-39 season as first choice and on 5 November scored twice in a 3-0 win over Stoke. A few weeks later, Gallacher, who scored 108 goals in 307 games for Sunderland, had joined the Potters but never really made his mark at the Victoria Ground.

GATES, ERIC

Eric Gates made his full first team debut for Ipswich Town at Derby County on 4 October 1975 after having made 13 appearances as a substitute. All Eric Gates' football with the Portman Road club was played in the First Division, though it was 1977-78 before he established himself as a first team regular. Two seasons later, Gates netted his first hat-trick for the club in a 4-0 home win over Manchester City whilst in the previous game, his strike in the 3-1 defeat of Southampton had been selected as the 'Goal of the Month' on the 'Match of the Day' television programme for November 1979.

Gates continued to find the net over the next two seasons in which Town finished runners-up in the First Division on both occasions. His form led to him winning two full caps for England, his first in the World Cup qualifying match against Norway at Wembley in 1981. Injuries hampered his progress in 1982-83 but over the next two seasons, he was the club's leading scorer. In the summer of 1985 after scoring 96 goals in 384 first team outings, he left Portman Road to join Sunderland.

He made his debut for the Wearsiders in a 2-0 home defeat by Blackburn Rovers on the opening day of the 1985-86 campaign and over the next five seasons was a first team regular. His best season for the club was undoubtedly the Third Division Championship-winning season of 1987-88 when he scored 20 goals including four in a 7-0 win over Southend United and a hat-trick in a 3-0 defeat of Rotherham United. He went on to score 55 goals in 236 League and Cup appearances before leaving the Wearsiders in the summer of 1990 to end his career with Carlisle United.

GEMMELL, JIMMY

Sunderland brought Jimmy Gemmell to Roker Park from Clyde in November 1900 and he made his first team debut for the Wearsiders in a 1-0 win over Sheffield Wednesday on 8 December 1900. A smart inside-forward who could play in any forward position, Gemmell won a League Championship medal with Sunderland in 1901-02 when he scored 10 goals in 31 league games. He continued to find the net with great regularity but in May 1907 he left the Wearsiders to join Stoke. He only stayed with the Potters for six months, and in November he joined Leeds United for family reasons.

He was eventually transferred back to Sunderland and took his tally of goals to 46 in 227 League and Cup appearances before leaving a second time to join Third Lanark in April 1912. The Glasgow-born utility forward had appeared in 290 league matches for his three English clubs and scored 62 goals.

GIANTKILLERS

Though Sunderland's 1-0 victory over Leeds United in the FA Cup Final of 1973 was the biggest upset in the competition since Blackburn Rovers struggling against relegation defeated double-chasing Huddersfield Town in 1928, the Wearsiders have also been the victims.

On 29 January 1929, Sunderland who were lying eighth in the First Division travelled to play Yeovil Town who were sixth from the foot of the Southern League. The Wearsiders were out-run and out-fought as Stock put Yeovil ahead after half-an-hour. Sunderland managed to equalise and force extra-time but it merely postponed the inevitable, Bryant put Yeovil ahead and that was the way it stayed.

GILLESPIE, JAMES

Scottish international forward James Gillespie joined Sunderland from Renton and scored on his debut in a 4-3 home defeat by Wolverhampton Wanderers in what was only the club's second Football League game. That was his only first team appearance that season and as he failed to make a start in 1891-92 it was 1892-93 before he established himself in the side. That season he scored 12 goals in 23 league games as the club retained the League Championship it had won the previous campaign.

He won another League Championship medal in 1894-95 when he again netted 12 league goals including two in the opening game of the season as Derby County were defeated 8-0.

In 1896-97 Sunderland ended the season in 15th place and so along with Burnley from the First Division and Second Division clubs Notts County and Newton Heath, the Wearsiders were involved in a series of Test matches to decide promotion and relegation. After two draws and a defeat, Sunderland had to beat Newton Heath in their final match to preserve their First Division status. Gillespie scored both goals for the club in a 2-0 win to enable the club to remain in the top flight.

It was his last appearance in Sunderland colours, and at the end of that season, in which he had scored 51 goals in 149 League and Cup games, he returned north of the border to play for Third Lanark. It was whilst playing for the Scottish League club that he won his only cap against Wales in 1898.

GOALKEEPERS

Sunderland FC has almost always been extremely well served by its goal-keepers and most of them have been very popular with the supporters. Ned Doig was the first in a long line of notable goalkeepers. He was ever-present in seven seasons and won four League Championship medals. After playing in 456 games, he joined Liverpool.

Dr Leigh Richmond Roose was a Welsh international goalkeeper who appeared in 99 games for the club and was one of the most famous ama-teur players of his day.

Joe Butler joined the club from Glossop and in his first season helped the club win the League Championship. Short and stocky, he was also in goal when Sunderland lost 1-0 to Aston Villa in the FA Cup Final that season.

Albert McInroy kept goal for the club between 1923 and 1929 and made 227 first team appearances, winning an England cap against North-ern Ireland in October 1926. Johnny Mapson joined the club from Read-ing and appeared in 385 games including being ever-present in 1946-47, the first season of peacetime football following the Second World War. During the hostilities he won England international honours.

Probably the greatest goalkeeper to represent the club is Jim Mont-gomery who appeared in a club record 623 games. Without doubt his greatest moment came in the club's 1973 FA Cup Final success over Leeds United when he first saved Trevor Cherry's diving header and then as the ball broke loose, dived back across his goal to push the ball up onto the crossbar before Dick Malone cleared the danger.

Over the next few seasons the club had four good 'keepers in the shape of Barry Siddall, Chris Turner, Iain Hesford and Tony Norman, all of whom gave the Wearsiders great service. Lionel Perez joined Sunderland from Bordeaux in the summer of 1996 and in his two seasons with the club turned in a number of impressive displays.

GOALS

The most goals Sunderland have ever scored in one game was their 23-0 victory over Castletown in what was supposedly a Durham Challenge Cup match which was later changed to a friendly. However, in a competitive match, the 11-1 FA Cup victory over Fairfields on 2 February 1895 remains the club record, whilst the 9-1 win over Newcastle United on 5 December 1908 is the Wearsiders' best result in the Football League.

GOALS - CAREER BEST
The highest goalscorer in the club's history is Bob Gurney, who between 1925 and 1939 netted 228 goals for the club. These comprised 205 league goals and 23 FA Cup goals.

GOALS - INDIVIDUAL
The most goals scored by a Sunderland player in any one match is five. This feat has been achieved by four players, the first being Jimmy Millar in the club's 11-2 FA Cup first round victory over non-League Fairfield on 2 February 1895.

The first player to achieve the feat in the Football League was Charlie Buchan on 7 December 1912 when Sunderland beat Liverpool 7-0 at Roker Park. The club's leading scorer in League and Cup matches, Bob Gurney netted five goals in Sunderland's 7-2 home win over Bolton Wanderers on 7 December 1935. The last Sunderland player to achieve this feat was Nick Sharkey in the 7-1 win over Norwich City on 20 March 1963.

GOALS - SEASON
The club's highest league goalscorer in any one season remains Dave Halliday who scored 43 league goals as Sunderland finished fourth in Division One in 1928-29. He scored all four goals in a 4-4 home draw against Sheffield United and hat-tricks against Derby County (Home 4-0), Manchester United (Home 5-1) and West Ham United (Home 4-1).

GOALSCORING RECORDS
Not since 1935-36 when Raich Carter and Bob Gurney each hit 31 goals in Division One for Sunderland, has any club in the top flight had two players with 30 or more goals in a season's league football.

In 1976-77 Sunderland went 10 games without scoring a goal, then won the next four games, scoring 17 goals!

GOODMAN, DON
Leeds-born forward Don Goodman played his early football with Collingham before entering league football with Bradford City. He had scored 22 goals in 86 games for the Valley Parade club and helped them win the

Third Division Championship when he joined West Bromwich Albion for £50,000 in March 1987. At the Hawthorns Goodman continued to score on a regular basis and had netted 63 in 181 League and Cup games when Sunderland paid £900,000 for his services in December 1991.

He made his debut for the north-east club on 7 December 1991, a day after putting pen to paper, in a 1-0 defeat at Wolverhampton Wanderers. On 11 January 1992, in only his seventh game for the club, he netted a hat-trick in a 6-2 home win over Millwall. After 11 goals in 22 games that season, he continued to find the net with great regularity and had scored 47 goals in 133 first team outings by the time of his £1.1 million move to Wolverhampton Wanderers in December 1994.

Don Goodman

On his arrival at Molineux he found himself playing behind Steve Bull and David Kelly but after replacing the Republic of Ireland international, he demonstrated his goalscoring talents with ten goals in a 13 match spell in 1995-96. In April 1996 he fractured his skull but made a remarkable recovery to return to first team action. He scored the winning goal against Leeds United in the quarter-final of the 1997-98 FA Cup competition and looked most likely to score against Arsenal in the semi-final before surprisingly being released in the summer after scoring 39 goals in 154 games for the Molineux club.

GRAINGER, COLIN

Wakefield-born player Colin Grainger, the 'singing winger', a well known crooner on the Northern pub and club circuit, began his career with Wrexham, turning professional in 1950. In July 1953 he joined Sheffield United for a fee of £2,500 and it was whilst at Bramall Lane that he won the first of seven England caps, netting twice on his debut in a 4-2 win over Brazil at Wembley. He had scored 26 goals in 88 league games for the Blades when Sunderland signed him in February 1957 for £7,000.

He made his debut for the Wearsiders in a 5-2 defeat at Tottenham Hotspur and over the next three seasons missed very few games. Despite the club being relegated to the Second Division for the first time in their history in 1957-58, Grainger was one of Sunderland's better players that season, his performances earning him his final cap against Scotland at Wembley. After scoring 14 goals in 124 games he joined Leeds United for £15,000 in August 1960.

The fast, direct winger failed to find his form at Elland Road and within 14 months had signed for Port Vale. Injuries restricted his appearances for the Valiants and he moved to Doncaster Rovers before ending his career with Macclesfield Town.

GRAY, FRANK

A former Parkhead ball-boy, Frank Gray went to Leeds United in the summer of 1970 after the Yorkshire club signed him in the face of stiff competition from a number of other clubs. He turned professional in 1971 and scored on his full debut in a 4-0 home win over Crystal Palace. After winning five Scottish Under-23 caps, he won the first of 32 full caps when he played against England at St James' Park in March 1974.

In July 1979 he moved to Nottingham Forest for a then Leeds club record fee of £500,000. Under Brian Clough, Gray enjoyed the best years of his career. He went on to play in 118 League and Cup games in two seasons at the City Ground. He won a European Cup winners' medal in 1980 to go with the runners-up one he won with Leeds United in 1975.

He returned to Elland Road in May 1981 and was Scotland's left-back in the 1982 World Cup in Spain.

Gray had played in 405 first team games for Leeds when in 1985 he was transferred by his brother to Sunderland. He played his first game for the Wearsiders in a 2-0 home defeat by Blackburn Rovers on the opening day of the 1985-86 campaign and over the next four seasons was a virtual ever-present, appearing in 146 league games. After helping the club win promotion from the Third Division in 1987-88, his experience proved an important factor during the following campaign as the club consolidated their position in the Second Division.

He was later appointed player-assistant manager of Darlington and after scouting for a number of clubs, became manager of Harrogate Town before taking charge of Al Manamah in Bahrain.

GRAY, MICHAEL

Sunderland-born Michael Gray joined his home-town club as a trainee and worked his way through the ranks to make his first team debut against Barnsley in December 1992, scoring the opening goal in a 2-1 win. After three seasons of being a fringe player, he was ever-present in 1995-96 as the club won the First Division Championship. Also, during that campaign he represented a Football League Under-21 XI against an Italian Serie 'B' side and was chosen by his fellow professionals as a member of the PFA First Division Select XI. Though not a prolific scorer, the goals he has scored have often been spectacular efforts and perhaps none more so than the 30-yard screamer against Birmingham City in April 1996.

He continued to impress in the Premier League even though he switched from his usual position on the left-side of midfield to left-back to accommodate Chris Waddle. He continued in this position in 1997-98, forming a good understanding with Allan Johnston down the club's left flank.

Michael Gray is a player of undoubted class and showed great strength of character in 1998-99 to overcome his penalty miss against Charlton Athletic in the play-off final to help the Wearsiders win the First Division title. His form during that Championship-winning season led to him winning full international honours for England.

GRAY, PHIL

Strong-running striker Phil Gray began his league career with Tottenham Hotspur and made his debut in the virtual reserve team that fulfilled a fixture at Everton five days before the 1987 FA Cup Final. After that he failed to make much of an impact mainly due to numerous injury problems that sidelined him for lengthy spells. He was loaned out to Barnsley and Fulham before being allowed to join Luton Town for £275,000 in August 1991.

Within a month of his arrival at Kenilworth Road, Gray had been elevated to Northern Ireland's full international squad, though he had to wait until 1993 before winning the first of 20 caps. The Belfast-born forward again suffered from injuries but after scoring 26 goals in 65 games for the Hatters he was transferred to Sunderland for a fee of £800,000 in the summer of 1993.

He made his debut for the Wearsiders in a 1-0 defeat at Notts County in the third game of the 1993-94 season and ended the campaign as the club's leading scorer with 14 league goals. He was the top goalscorer again the following season but in 1995-96 was injured during February and missed out on the title run-in.

He thoroughly deserved his First Division Championship medal. Before his injury he had scored nine goals including a 30-yard piledriver in the 4-0 win over Grimsby Town. At the end of that season, Gray who had scored 41 goals in 132 games became a free agent and joined Nancy. He later played for Fortuna Sittard before rejoining Luton Town for £400,000 in September 1997. Injuries have since impaired his performances.

GUEST PLAYERS

The 'Guest' system was used by all clubs during the two wars. Although at times it was abused almost beyond belief (in that some sides that opposed Sunderland had ten or eleven guests!) it normally worked sensibly and effectively to the benefit of the players, clubs and supporters.

Sunderland had many 'guests' during both wars who were, or later became international players. These included Jimmy Seed, Jackie Milburn and Stan Mortensen. Another player to 'guest' for the Wearsiders was Harry Potts who went on to play in 181 games for Burnley before managing the Turf Moor club for 14 years.

GURNEY, BOB

Bob Gurney scored a record 228 League and Cup goals for Sunderland after starting his career with Hetton Juniors and Bishop Auckland. He arrived at Roker Park in 1925 and in his first competitive game, scored nine goals for Sunderland reserves against Hartlepool United. He made his first team debut on 3 April 1926, scoring for the Wearsiders in a 3-2 defeat at West Ham United. However, he was kept out of a regular place by Dave Halliday until 1929-30 when he finished the campaign as the club's leading scorer.

He had scored his first hat-trick for the club in a 5-1 home win over Arsenal in March 1928 but surprisingly did not play in a single game the following season as Halliday scored 43 goals. In 1929-30, the season that Gurney established himself as first team regular, he scored four goals at Anfield as Sunderland beat Liverpool 6-0. Liverpool were Sunderland's opponents in 1930-31 when Gurney scored a hat-trick in a 6-5 win at Roker Park. That season he netted another threesome in a 5-1 win over Sheffield Wednesday to end the campaign with 33 goals in 45 games.

The Yorkshire side were on the receiving end of another Gurney treble the following season. In 1932-33, Gurney scored four goals in a 7-4 home win over Bolton Wanderers and a hat-trick in a 3-0 FA Cup Cup fourth round victory over Aston Villa. His next hat-trick in March 1934 came in an eleven-goal thriller at The Hawthorns as Sunderland lost 6-5 to West Bromwich Albion. In 1934-35 he scored 34 goals in 43 games including a hat-trick in a 3-0 win at Stoke's Victoria Ground.

The following season, Gurney netted 31 goals in 39 league games as Sunderland won the League Championship including five against Bolton Wanderers as the Lancashire club were beaten 7-2 and four in a similar scoreline as the Wearsiders defeated Birmingham at St Andrews.

In 1937 his equaliser proved the turning point in the FA Cup Final against Preston North End as Sunderland went on to win 3-1.

He made one appearance for England against Scotland in 1935 but four years later his career ended when he broke his leg after just two minutes of an FA Cup tie with Blackburn Rovers. Gurney actually hobbled back onto the pitch before the full extent of the injury was diagnosed.

He later managed Peterborough United in their Midland League days but had little success at either Darlington or Hartlepool United both of whom he managed at a later date.

H

HALL, ALEX

Full-back Alex Hall began his career with Scottish League club Dunfermline Athletic before joining Sunderland in April 1929. He made his debut for the then Roker Park club in the penultimate game of the season as the Wearsiders went down 4-0 at Sheffield United. Over the next four seasons he only appeared in 31 league games despite being able to play in both right and left-back positions as Bill Murray and Harold Shaw established themselves as the club's first-choice pairing.

In 1934-35 he not only won a regular place in the Sunderland defence but scored his only goal for the club in 10 seasons at Roker Park in a 3-0 home win over Leeds United.

He won a League Championship medal in 1935-36 and an FA Cup winners' medal the following season when the Wearsiders beat Preston North End 3-1.

Hall appeared in 236 games for the north-east club before returning to Scotland at the end of the Second World War to end his career with Hibernian.

HALL, FRED

Chester-le-Street-born Fred Hall was a full-back with Blackburn Rovers from November 1935 and a wartime 'guest' for Arsenal, Norwich City and Tottenham Hotspur. During the war years, this tall commanding figure moved to centre-half and proved a valuable asset to all of his wartime clubs.

In August 1946 he joined Sunderland after making 29 league appearances for the Ewood Park club and made his debut for the Wearsiders in a 3-2 home win over Derby County on the opening day of the 1946-47 season. Over the next nine seasons he missed very few matches and was everpresent in 1951-52. Playing all of his games for Sunderland in the top flight, his only goal for the club came on Christmas Day 1953 when he scored the Wearsider's goal in a 1-1 home draw against Huddersfield Town.

Fred Hall came close to international recognition which he probably would have achieved had he not lost his best years to the war. He played in 224 games for Sunderland before moving to Barrow where he finished his senior career after just one season.

HALLIDAY, DAVE

Dave Halliday was born in Dumfries and in his teens was soon attracting a number of Scottish clubs. He began his career with his local side Queen of the South before later playing for St Mirren and then Dundee. At Dens Park he created the club scoring record when in 1923-24 he netted 38 goals.

During the summer of 1925, Sunderland paid £4,000 for his goalscoring skills as they sought an immediate replacement for Charlie Buchan who had joined Arsenal.

He scored two goals on his debut in a 3-1 home win over Birmingham on the opening day of the 1925-26 season and in fact, scored 10 goals in his first four games including hat-tricks against West Bromwich Albion (Away 5-2) and Sheffield United (Home 6-1). He ended the season as the club's top scorer with 42 League and Cup goals including another treble in the 8-1 FA Cup win over non-League Boston. In his next season with the club he scored four goals in a 6-1 win over Manchester United, a club against whom he always seemed to score, and hat-tricks against Burnley (Home 7-1) West Bromwich Albion (Home 4-1) and Leeds United (Home 6-2).

In 1927-28 Halliday scored in each of the first eight games of the season including a hat-trick in a 5-3 defeat at Bury. Once again top scoring with 37 goals in 41 League and Cup games, he netted another hat-trick against Manchester United in a 4-1 home win and four goals in a 5-3 defeat of Portsmouth at Fratton Park.

In 1928-29 he established a new club scoring record, netting 43 goals in 38 league games including all four in a 4-4 home draw against Sheffield United and hat-tricks against Derby County (Home 4-0)

Manchester United (Home 5-1) and West Ham United (Home 4-1).

After netting a hat-trick against Manchester City at the start of the 1929-30 season, Halliday played his last game for the club at Sheffield United before joining Arsenal for £6,500. In all he scored 162 goals in only 175 League and Cup games for the Wearsiders. Only Bob Gurney and Charlie Buchan have scored more for the club.

He never really settled at Highbury, though he did score four for the Gunners against Leicester City and after 12 months he had joined Manchester City. At Maine Road he rediscovered his goalscoring touch, hitting 47 goals in only 76 games. When he turned out for City against Sunderland in January 1932 he scored an eight-minute hat-trick against his former club as the Wearsiders lost 5-2.

After hanging up his boots he took charge of Yeovil Town for a spell before becoming manager of Aberdeen. He had an excellent period in charge of the Dons, reaching six Cup Finals and winning the Scottish League Championship in his 17 years at Pittodrie. In 1955 he joined Leicester City and led them to the Second Division Championship before leaving Filbert Street in 1959.

Though never recognised by Scotland, he was one of the most popular players ever to play for Sunderland. Once against Arsenal he had given Lewis the Gunners' 'keeper a constant battering throughout the game and towards full-time was involved in a free-for-all in the goalmouth. Sent-off with Lewis, he was given a standing ovation by the Roker crowd!

HALOM, VIC

Vic Halom was an aggressive and bustling striker who began his Football League career with Charlton Athletic before joining Leyton Orient. Fulham manager Bobby Robson just beat Brian Clough for his signature when he signed the solidly-built forward for a fee of £35,000 in November 1968. At Craven Cottage he helped the club win promotion to the Second Division in 1971 and scored 22 goals in 72 league games before signing for Luton Town. After a similar goalscoring record with the Hatters, 17 goals in 59 games, he moved to Sunderland in February 1973 and made his debut for the Wearsiders in a 1-0 defeat at Sheffield Wednesday. By the end of that season, Halom had won an FA Cup winners' medal as Sunderland surprisingly beat Leeds United in the 1973 Final after scoring one of the goals in the 2-1 semi-final win over Arsenal.

In 1973-74 Halom scored 21 goals in 48 League and Cup games

including a hat-trick in a 3-0 League Cup second round second replay win over Derby County. He also helped the Wearsiders win promotion as Second Division champions in 1975-76 before leaving to join Oldham Athletic. The popular striker had scored 40 goals in 134 first team outings for Sunderland and his departure was not welcomed by most of the club's supporters.

In his first season at Boundary Park, he was the club's leading scorer with 18 goals in 37 league games but in February 1980 he moved across the Pennines to end his career with Rotherham United where he played a number of games in a central midfield role.

After managing non-League Barrow, he took charge of Rochdale but failing to find success returned to non-League circles, first as manager of Burton Albion and then North Shields.

HANNAH, DAVID

Inside-forward David Hannah was on the books of the Scottish side Renton when they won the Scottish Cup in 1888, before joining Sunderland in their first-ever league season of 1890-91. He was ever-present in that campaign and went on to enjoy great success in his four seasons with the Wearsiders. He helped them win the League Championship in 1891-92 and 1892-93, to the runners-up spot in 1893-94 and to an FA Cup semi-final in 1891-92. He had scored 25 goals in 89 games when he was transferred to Liverpool in 1894.

He spent three years with the Anfield club, helping them win promotion to the First Division after winning the Second Division Championship.

In 1895-96 he moved on to Dundee before joining Woolwich Arsenal in October 1897. At the end of his first season with the London club he was joint-top scorer with 12 goals including a hat-trick in a 4-2 win over Small Heath on 5 March 1898. He went on to appear in 50 League and Cup games for Arsenal before hanging up his boots.

HANNAH, JOHN

After starting his career with Third Lanark where he was capped for Scotland against Wales in 1889, he joined Sunderland Albion before being transferred to the Wearsiders in January 1891. He had to wait until the fifth game of the following season before making his debut in a 2-1 home win over Everton and ended the campaign with 20 goals in 27 League and Cup games when the club won the League Championship for the first time. Sunderland retained the title in 1892-93 with Hannah again netting 20 goals including a hat-trick in a 5-2 defeat of Wolverhampton Wanderers. After helping the club finish runners-up the following campaign he was in particularly good form in 1894-95 when the club won their third league title in four seasons, netting a hat-trick in a 4-4 draw at home to Aston Villa and another in the club's biggest FA Cup victory, 11-1 over non-League Fairfields.

Hannah went on to score 77 goals in 172 games in his six seasons with the club before returning north of the border to end his career with his first club, Third Lanark.

HARDWICK, GEORGE

England's captain in the immediate post-war years, George Hardwick was a born leader who captained every team for which he played. A cultured and immaculate defender, he began his career with Middlesbrough for whom he played in 143 league games. During the Second World War he appeared in two wartime Cup Finals as 'guest' for Chelsea, but in November 1950 he left Ayresome Park to become player-manager of Oldham Athletic.

He exerted great influence on the Boundary Park side and in 1952-53 led the club to the Third Division (North) championship. However, the Latics were relegated the following season as he had no money to strengthen the side. After a poor season in 1955-56, Hardwick left the club and did not return to management for eight years.

He became Sunderland's manager in November 1964 but his spell in charge of the club was very brief. In his first match in charge, the Reds beat Burnley at Roker Park 3-2 to record only their second victory of the season. However, the club struggled to avoid relegation to the Second Division and eventually finished in 15th position. The supporters and the board expected more and at the end of the season, he lost his job. He then became manager of Gateshead but had an unhappy time there as well, when in 1969-70 they lost their Northern Premier League status.

Sunderland's full league record under George Hardwick is:

P	W	D	L	F	A
42	14	9	19	64	74

HARRIS, GORDON

After impressing for Nottinghamshire Schoolboys, Gordon Harris was working down the pit and representing his colliery when he was recommended to Burnley in 1957. He scored on his First Division debut at home to Leeds United in January 1959 but only appeared occasionally in the first team when the Clarets won that season's League Championship.

After Brian Pilkington had joined Bolton Wanderers, Harris established himself in the Burnley first team and in November 1961 won his first representative honours when he was selected for the Football League against the Irish League. He scored in a 6-1 victory and a week later represented the England Under-23 side against Israel at Elland Road. He won his only full England cap in a 1-1 draw with Poland at Goodison Park in January 1966 and though he was chosen in Alf Ramsey's initial World Cup squad of 40, he failed to make the tournament itself.

Appointed Burnley's club captain for the 1967-68 season, Harris was dropped and disciplined just before Christmas 1967 and shortly afterwards joined Sunderland for a record £70,000.

He made his debut on 3 February 1968 in a 1-0 win at Sheffield Wednesday and became a regular member of the Sunderland side replacing the great Jim Baxter until losing his first team place in 1971. Harris who had scored 16 goals in 136 outings for the Wearsiders retired from league football and joined non-League South Shields where he played out his career.

HARVEY, MARTIN

Belfast-born Martin Harvey was a stylish and constructive wing-half who worked his way up through the ranks before making his first team debut in a goalless draw at Plymouth Argyle on 24 October 1959. Over the next four seasons, Harvey only appeared in 23 league games but did score his first goal for the club in a 2-1 win at Luton Town in April 1962. After establishing himself in the club's midfield during the Second Division promotion-winning season of 1963-64, replacing Stan Anderson, he went on to be a virtual ever-present for the next nine seasons.

Having won honours for Northern Ireland at schoolboy, Under-23 and 'B' international level, he won the first of his 34 full caps in 1961 when he played against Italy, and his last ten years later, against Wales.

A fine tackler and an excellent all-round player, he went on to appear in 361 League and Cup games for Sunderland before becoming assistant-manager of Carlisle United. He later took over from Bobby Moncur as the Brunton Park club's manager and as results improved, the club eventually finished sixth in 1979-80. However, after a very bad start to the following season, Harvey resigned and was thus, the shortest ever serving manager of Carlisle United.

HASTINGS, ALEX

Wing-half Alex Hastings joined the Wearsiders from Scottish League club Stenhousemuir in the summer of 1930 and made his debut in the third game of the 1930-31 season after the first two games had ended all-square at 3-3. Hastings' debut against Portsmouth at Fratton Park on 6 September 1930 also ended level at 1-1. He played in 30 league games that season and was a first team regular for nine seasons up until the outbreak of the Second World War.

After helping the Wearsiders win the League Championship in 1935-36, he won the first of two full caps for Scotland when he was selected to play against Northern Ireland in Belfast, a match which the Scots won 3-1. He returned to the Irish capital two years later and was again on the winning side.

During the war years he appeared in 106 wartime games but retired in May 1946 after playing in a total of 303 League and Cup games for the club. Captain of the 1935-36 League Championship winning side, most of his eight goals for Sunderland came when he was asked to play at centre-forward for the club during an emergency, though he did score in two of the three games played at the start of the aborted 1939-40 campaign.

HAT-TRICKS

Sunderland players have netted 157 hat-tricks in Football League games with Dave Halliday holding the club record having scored 14, closely followed by Bob Gurney with 11.

Johnny Campbell scored the club's first hat-trick in the Football League on 25 October 1890 in a 5-2 win at Bolton Wanderers.

Only two Sunderland players have scored a hat-trick on their debut for the club. The first to achieve the feat was Ronnie Turnbull who netted all four goals in a 4-1 home win over Portsmouth on 29 November 1947. John Hawley scored a hat-trick on his debut for the club on 6 October 1979 when Charlton Athletic were beaten 4-0.

There have been seven occasions when two Sunderland players have scored hat-tricks in the same match. The first came in the FA Cup first round victory over Fairfield in 1894-95 when five goals from Jimmy Millar and three from John Hannah helped Sunderland to an 11-1 win. The first instance in the Football League came the following season when Johnny

Campbell and Jimmy Millar scored three goals apiece in a 7-1 home win over West Bromwich Albion. In 1908-09, Billy Hogg and George Holley each scored a hat-trick in Sunderland's surprise 9-1 victory over rivals Newcastle United at St James' Park. When Boston were beaten 8-1 in the third round of the FA Cup in January 1926, Bob Kelly and Dave Halliday both scored hat-tricks. The following season, Halliday and Steve Coglin netted three goals apiece in a 7-1 victory over Burnley. Another Lancashire club, Blackburn Rovers were beaten 8-2 in February 1931 with Billy Eden and Jimmy Leonard scoring hat-tricks. The last occasion when two Sunderland players scored hat-tricks in the same match occurred on 9 December 1961 when Brian Clough and Ambrose Fogarty achieved the feat in a 7-2 home win over Swansea Town.

At the time of writing, the last Sunderland player to score a hat-trick is Niall Quinn in a 4-1 win over Stockport County on 7 March 1998.

HEDLEY, JACK

Full-back Jack Hedley played his early football with Willington Quay before making his Football League debut for Everton in a 3-0 home win over Aston Villa in September 1947. He went on to appear in 61 first team games in three seasons at Goodison Park before being transferred to Sunderland for a fee of £10,000 in the summer of 1950.

His first game in the red and white stripes of Sunderland came on 23 December 1950 in a 2-1 home win over Liverpool. After that, he missed very few games and was ever-present in seasons 1954-55 and 1956-57. Though he possessed a powerful long range shot, Hedley never got on the scoresheet for the Wearsiders in nine seasons with the club. Hedley, who also had a spell playing for Millionairos in Bogota, went on to appear in 295 League and Cup games for Sunderland before leaving to end his League career with Gateshead in June 1959.

HERD, GEORGE

Scottish international George Herd began his career with Clyde, where he was capped five times at full level before being transferred to Sunderland in April 1961 for a fee of £42,500. He made his debut for the club in the final game of the 1960-61 season in a 1-1 home draw against Liverpool.

Over the next eight seasons, Herd was a virtual ever-present in the Sunderland side, creating a great number of chances for Brian Clough as well as netting his fair share himself. His best season in terms of goals scored was

1963-64 when the club won promotion to the First Division, Herd netting 13 in 39 games.

On 7 January 1967, Herd became the first Sunderland substitute to score when he netted in the 1-1 draw against Blackpool at Bloomfield Road.

He went on to score 55 goals in 326 League and Cup games for the Wearsiders before retiring at the end of the 1968-69 season. The following summer he made a return to league action with Hartlepool United but after 13 appearances, decided to retire again.

HESFORD, IAIN

Kenya-born goalkeeper Iain Hesford is the son of Bob Hesford who kept goal for Huddersfield Town in the 1938 FA Cup Final.

Iain Hesford joined Blackpool as an apprentice in August 1977 and understudied George Wood until the Scottish international 'keeper signed for Everton. Hesford made his Football League debut for the Seasiders in a 1-1 draw at home to Oldham Athletic on the opening day of the 1977-78 campaign. In just over five seasons at Bloomfield Road, Hesford played in 230 League and Cup games before leaving to join Sheffield Wednesday in August 1983.

Unable to break into the first team at Hillsborough he had loan spells with Fulham and Notts County until Lawrie McMenemy signed him for Sunderland in the summer of 1986 for a fee of £80,000.

Iain Hesford

After making his debut in a 2-0 win at Huddersfield Town on the opening day of the 1986-87 season, Hesford turned in a number of memorable performances in a campaign in which he was ever-present. The Wearsiders were relegated to the Third Division, but in 1987-88 with Hesford keeping 13 clean sheets in his 39 appearances, the club won the Championship and an immediate return to the Second Division.

After appearing in 114 first team games, Hesford left Roker Park to join Hull City. He later returned to Bloomfield Road before ending his league career with Maidstone United.

HINDMARCH, ROB

A strong defender, hard in the tackle, Rob Hindmarch began his career with Sunderland, whom he joined straight from school in the summer of 1976. An England Youth international, he made his first team debut for the Wearsiders in a 2-2 draw at Orient in January 1978. After helping the club win promotion to the First Division in 1979-80, Hindmarch went on to play in 132 games for the club before leaving to play for Derby County after a brief spell on loan with Portsmouth. His only goal for Sunderland came in a 5-0 League Cup win over Wolverhampton Wanderers during the 1982-83 competition.

Rob Hindmarch

He slotted into the Rams' line-up well and played nearly 200 games for them, gaining a Second Division Championship medal in 1986-87 before moving to Wolverhampton Wanderers for a fee of £350,000. After a successful first season with the Molineux club, injuries hampered his progress and he was allowed to join Gillingham where he ended his league career without making a first team appearance.

HOBSON, BERT

Full-back Bert Hobson who was at home playing on either flank, joined Sunderland from non-League Crook Town in the summer of 1912. Though he only appeared in three games for the club during the following League Championship-winning season as a replacement for Charlie Gladwin, he was always on the winning side - Sheffield United (Away 3-1) Everton (Home 3-1) and Liverpool (Away 5-2).

For five seasons either side of the First World War, Hobson was a first team regular and in 1919 played in all but two of the Victory League games, scoring his only ever goal for the club in a 2-0 home win over Middlesbrough. He went on to play in 172 League and Cup games for the Wearsiders before being allowed to leave Roker Park in March 1922 and join Rochdale.

HOGG, BILLY

Inside-forward Billy Hogg joined Sunderland from Willington in October 1899 but had to wait a couple of months before making his debut, scoring one of the Wearsiders' goals in a 5-0 win over Notts County. In the Championship-winning season of 1901-02, Hogg was the club's top scorer with ten goals, his form gaining him three international caps.

Hogg was a well-built player but was nevertheless noted for his speed and ball skills. His best season in terms of goals scored was 1903-04 when he found the net 13 times in 33 outings. He served Sunderland well, playing in 302 games and scoring 85 goals in his ten seasons. In his last season at Roker Park, Hogg scored the only two hat-tricks of his Sunderland career in successive away games - Woolwich Arsenal (4-1 on 8 November 1908) and Newcastle United (9-1 on 5 December 1908).

He left Sunderland in the summer of 1909 and joined Glasgow Rangers where his career took on a new lease of life. He found Scottish League success with the Ibrox club in 1911, 1912 and 1913.

HOLLEY, GEORGE

George Holley who was a supreme dribbler and entertainer was also both scorer and provider. He joined the club from Seaham White Star and scored Sunderland's goal on his debut in a 1-1 draw at Sheffield Wednesday on 27 December 1904. He also netted on his home debut four days later as Preston North End were beaten 3-2.

It was the 1907-08 season before he established himself in the Sunderland side, scoring 22 goals in 35 league games including hat-tricks against Nottingham Forest (Home 7-2) and Blackburn Rovers (Home 4-0). The following season he netted another hat-trick as Sunderland beat Newcastle United 9-1 at St James' Park. It was this kind of form that led to him winning full international honours against Wales in March 1909.

Holley went on to score eight goals in 10 international appearances for his country. Further hat-tricks followed in 1909-10 as Woolwich Arsenal were beaten 6-2 and Chelsea 4-0, both in front of Roker Park crowds that were not being treated to an exciting style of football at the time. On 4 February 1911, Holley scored all four goals in a 4-1 win over Bury and repeated the feat early the following season as Manchester United were beaten 5-0. Also during that 1911-12 campaign which was his best in terms of goals scored as he netted 25 in 32 league games, he hit another hat-trick in a 4-0 home win over Everton.

In 1912-13, Holey won a League Championship medal with the Wearsiders and netted another three goals in a 5-1 win at Bradford City. The following season he scored 15 goals in 16 games including hat-tricks in two home wins over Bolton Wanderers (3-2) and Everton (5-2).

He had scored 154 goals in 315 League and Cup games when he was allowed to leave Roker Park and join Brighton and Hove Albion in the summer of 1919.

HOME MATCHES
Sunderland's best home wins are the 11-1 win over Fairfield in the FA Cup competition of 1894-95 and the 9-0 defeat of Chatham in 1913-14 also in the FA Cup. In the league, Sunderland beat Derby County 8-0 in September 1894 and have scored eight goals in home matches on a further four occasions - West Bromwich Albion (8-1 in 1892-93); Boston (8-1 in the FA Cup competition of 1925-26); Blackburn Rovers (8-2 in 1930-31) and Charlton Athletic (8-1 in 1956-57). The club's worst home defeat is 6-1, a scoreline inflicted upon the club by Newcastle United on Boxing Day 1955.

HOME SEASONS
Sunderland have gone through a complete league season with an undefeated home record on six occasions, 1891-92, 1892-93, 1894-95, 1895-96,

1975-76 and 1979-80. In 1891-92, the Wearsiders won all 13 of their home matches in winning the League Championship, whilst the club's highest number of home wins in a league season is 19. This was achieved in 1975-76 from 21 matches when the club won the Second Division Championship.

HONOURS
The major honours achieved by the club are:

Division One Champions	1891-92	1892-93	1894-95
	1901-02	1912-13	1935-36
	1995-96	1998-99	
Division One Runners-Up	1893-94	1897-98	1900-01
	1922-23	1934-35	
Division Two Champions	1975-76		
Division Two Runners-Up	1963-64	1979-80	
Division Three Champions	1987-88		
FA Cup Winners	1937	1973	
FA Cup Runners-Up	1913	1992	
League Cup Runners-Up	1985		

HUDGELL, ARTHUR
Arthur Hudgell joined Crystal Palace from Eton Manor in December 1937, although he did not make his first team debut for the Selhurst Park club until Palace were playing in wartime regional football. He became a first team regular in the first post-war season of 1946-47 but when Palace played in an FA Cup tie at Newcastle, a Sunderland scout was impressed by Hudgell's performance and in January 1947 he signed for the Wearsiders for £10,000, then a record fee for a full-back.

He made his debut in a 2-1 win at Blackburn Rovers on 1 February 1947 and over the next eight seasons was a virtual ever-present in the Sunderland side. Hudgell played all his football for the north-east club in the First Division, amassing 275 League and Cup appearances. His last game in Sunderland's colours came in the final match of the 1956-57 season when the Reds lost 3-2 at Portsmouth.

HUGHES, BILLY
Brother of John, who was forced to quit the game through injury, Billy Hughes joined the Wearsiders from Coatbridge Juniors in December 1965.

After some impressive performances for the club's reserve side, he made his first team debut in a 2-2 draw at home to Liverpool on 4 February 1967, making just a handful of appearances in his first few seasons with the club.

It was 1968-69 when he established himself as a regular member of the Sunderland side and for the next nine seasons missed very few games, being an ever-present in 1974-75.

Hughes' best season as a goalscorer was 1972-73 when he scored 19 goals in 43 League and Cup games. His total included a hat-trick in a 3-0 home win over Huddersfield Town and a goal in the 2-1 FA Cup semi-final win over Arsenal at Hillsborough that helped the Wearsiders into the final where they beat Leeds United. Hughes' other hat-trick for the club came in a 5-1 defeat of Bristol Rovers in September 1974 as he netted 15 goals in the 1974-75 ever-present campaign. It was that kind of form that won him his sole international cap when he came on as a substitute for Scotland against Sweden in 1975. After helping the club win promotion to the First Division in 1975-76, Hughes was hampered by injuries and a loss of form, and in September 1977 after scoring 82 goals in 344 games, he was transferred to Derby County.

He never really settled at the Baseball Ground and after just four months, moved to Leicester City. He later had a loan spell with Carlisle United before leaving the game. He is now clubhouse manager and steward of the Stressholme Golf Club in Darlington.

Billy Hughes

HUNDRED GOALS

Sunderland have scored more than 100 league goals in a season on two occasions. The highest total is 109 goals scored in 1935-36 when they won the League Championship. The club first scored 100 goals in 1892-93 when they won the First Division title for the second year in succession.

HURLEY, CHARLIE

A living legend, Charlie Hurley was recently voted the club's best ever player. He came to England at the age of seven to live in Hornchurch and after being spotted by Bill Voisey, he signed for Millwall as a youngster. He had made 105 league appearances for the Lions, and had just won his first full cap for the Republic of Ireland in a World Cup qualifier against England when he left The Den to join Sunderland for a fee of £18,000 in September 1957.

His first game for the club could not have been worse as the Wearsiders lost 7-0 at Blackpool and Hurley put through his own goal! His next appearance in Sunderland colours wasn't much better as Burnley beat the then Roker Park club 6-0. Many of the Sunderland supporters must have wondered what sort of centre-half manager Alan Brown had signed. But they needn't have worried for Charlie Hurley proved himself over the next 12 seasons to be one of the best pivots in the country.

In 1958, he won the first of 38 caps he gained for the Republic of Ireland whilst with Sunderland, when he played against Denmark and later during his career, he became player-manager of his country.

He helped Sunderland back into the First Division in 1963-64 as they ended the season as runners-up to Leeds United. Known as 'King Charlie' he went on to play in 402 first team games for the club and though he only scored 26 goals, most of them were crucial strikes, like the all-important goal late on in the match against Norwich City in the fifth round of the FA Cup in February 1961.

In the summer of 1969, Hurley was given a free transfer by the board as a thank-you for the loyal service he had shown whilst with the club. He was allowed to negotiate his own contract, and he joined Bolton Wanderers. In two seasons with the Trotters, he appeared in 46 first team games.

In January 1972 he was appointed manager of Reading out of 50 applicants and took them to promotion for the first time in 50 years when they finished third in Division Four in 1975-76. Reading were relegated the following year and Hurley resigned, saying that the players were not responding to his methods of management.

I

INTERNATIONAL MATCHES
The first International match to be played at Roker Park was on 18 February 1899 when an England side containing Sunderland's Philip Bach beat Ireland 13-2 to record what is still England's record score. The two countries met again on 23 October 1920. England played host to Wales at Roker Park on 15 November 1950 and with Sunderland's Willie Watson in their side, won 4-2.

In the 1966 World Cup which was staged in this country, Roker Park hosted three Group Four games with the following results: Chile 0 Italy 2, Italy 0 USSR 1, Chile 1 USSR 2 - before USSR beat Hungary 2-1 in the quarter-final game watched by a crowd of 26,844.

INTERNATIONAL PLAYERS
Sunderland's most internationally capped player (ie: international caps gained while players were registered with the club) is Charlie Hurley with 38 caps. The following is a complete list of players who have gained full international honours for England, Scotland, Wales, Northern Ireland and the Republic of Ireland:

England		Scotland	
Stan Anderson	2	George Aitken	3
Philip Bach	1	Jim Baxter	10
Arthur Bridgett	11	Billy Clunas	2

England

Charlie Buchan	6
Raich Carter	6
Warney Cresswell	5
Frank Cuggy	2
Colin Grainger	1
Michael Gray	2
Bob Gurney	1
Billy Hogg	3
George Holley	10
Robert Kelly	1
Albert McInroy	1
Henry Martin	1
Jackie Mordue	2
Kevin Phillips	1
Nick Pickering	1
Tom Porteous	1
Len Shackleton	5
Tony Towers	3
Dave Watson	14

Scotland

John Connor	4
Ned Doig	3
Willie Fraser	2
Patsy Gallacher	1
Alex Hastings	2
Billy Hughes	1
Bert Johnstone	1
Andrew McCombie	2
Sandy McNab	1
George Mulhall	2
Tommy Tait	1
Charlie Thompson	9
Charlie Thomson	1
Jim Watson	4
Hugh Wilson	1
Tommy Wright	3

Northern Ireland

Willie Watson	4
Billy Bingham	33

Wales

Harry Buckle	1	Ray Daniel	9
Tom Finney	7	Trevor Ford	13
Phil Gray	13	Leighton James	1
Martin Harvey	34	Andy Melville	17
Ian Lawther	2	Colin Pascoe	8
English McConnell	4	Leigh Roose	9
Jimmy Nicholl	5	Willie Watkins	3
Jimmy O'Neill	1		

Republic of Ireland

John Park	11
John Byrne	2
John Feenan	2
Ambrose Fogarty	10

The first Sunderland player to be capped was Tom Porteous when he played for England v Wales in 1891.

Charlie Hurley	38
David Kelly	4
Niall Quinn	3

IRWIN, CECIL

England Schoolboy international full-back Cecil Irwin worked his way up through the ranks before making his first team debut in a 2-0 home defeat by Ipswich Town on 20 September 1958. It was his only appearance that season and though he only played in 10 league games in his first three seasons at Roker Park, he established himself as a first team regular in 1961-62.

In 1963-64 he was in outstanding form as the club won promotion to the First Division as runners-up to Leeds United, appearing in 39 of the club's 42 league games. His only goal for the club in 14 seasons of league football came on 12 October 1968 in a 3-1 home win over Nottingham Forest.

Irwin played the last of his 354 League and Cup games for the Wearsiders on 4 September 1971 as the north-east club drew 1-1 at Millwall. At the end of that season, Irwin left Roker Park to play non-League football for Yeovil Town.

ISLE OF MAN CUP

The club have entered this competition on two occasions, winning the trophy both times. In 1983, Sunderland won all three matches - Isle Of Man XI 5-1 at Castletown; Burnley 1-0 at Douglas and St Mirren 1-0 at Douglas. The club retained the trophy the following year, beating Carlisle United 2-1 at Ramsey; drawing 1-1 with Athlone Town at Douglas and then defeating Blackburn Rovers 1-0 also at Douglas.

J

JOHNSTON, BERT

Centre-half Bert Johnston joined the Wearsiders from Scottish junior side Alva Albion Rangers in the summer of 1929 and after working his way through the ranks, made his first team debut in a 3-0 win at West Ham United on 25 April 1931, replacing the injured Jock McDougall. He made seven league appearances in each of the following two seasons before staking a claim for a regular first team place in 1933-34. He won a League Championship medal in 1935-36 and the following season was a member of the Sunderland team that beat Preston North End 3-1 in the FA Cup Final at Wembley.

His consistent performances in the heart of the Sunderland defence saw him win full international honours for Scotland when he played against Czechoslovakia in 1938. He had appeared in 164 League and Cup games for the Wearsiders when war broke out in 1939 and the following year he retired and became the club's trainer.

JUBILEE FUND

The League Benevolent Fund was launched in 1938, fifty years after the start of the Football League, to benefit players who had fallen on hard times.

It was decided that the best way to raise funds was for sides to play local 'derby' games with no account being taken of league status. Sunderland travelled to Middlesbrough and drew 3-3 with Cliff Whitelum scoring two of their goals, before a disappointing attendance of 8,000.

K

KAY, JOHN

John Kay joined Arsenal as an apprentice in April 1980 before turning professional in July 1981. He started his career as a skilful midfield player but was converted to full-back after his promotion to the club's reserve team. He made his Football League debut against West Bromwich Albion in February 1983 but after making just 14 league appearances he was surprisingly released on a free transfer and joined Wimbledon. During three seasons with the Dons, he helped them win promotion and played in 70 first team games before joining Sunderland in the summer of 1987 for a fee of £22,500.

After making his debut in a 1-0 win at Brentford in the club's first-ever Division Three game, he was ever-present and won a Third Division Championship medal as the Wearsiders finished nine points ahead of runners-up Brighton and Hove Albion. He also helped the club win promotion to the First Division in 1989-90 and went on to appear in 236 League and Cup games before being given a free transfer in the summer of 1996 after a series of injury problems had limited his appearances.

He joined Preston North End for a month, covering for both injured full-backs before signing for Scarborough in September 1996. He made the right-back position his own and in 1997-98 was voted the club's Player of the Year after a season of consistent displays.

KERR, BOBBY

Dumbarton-born midfielder Bobby Kerr was a great servant to Sunderland

Football Club, scoring 67 goals in 436 League and Cup games in 12 seasons with the club. After working his way up through the junior teams, he made his full first team debut against Manchester City on 31 December 1966 and scored the only goal of the game. In fact, Kerr scored in each of his first four home appearances, following his strike with a goal in each game against Chelsea (2-0) and Liverpool (2-2) before netting twice in the 3-0 defeat of Newcastle United. Kerr's best season in terms of goals scored was 1971-72 when he netted 12 in 50 games.

Between seasons 1971-72 and 1975-76 Kerr missed just five games out of a possible 210 and was the club's captain when they won the FA Cup in 1973. He was in inspirational form in 1975-76 when the Wearsiders won the Second Division Championship, though he suffered from injuries during the club's top flight campaign. He left Roker Park in March 1979 to join Blackpool but things didn't work out for him at Bloomfield Road and 16 months later he moved to Hartlepool United where he ended his league career.

Bobby Kerr

KNIGHTON, KEN

Ken Knighton developed into a fine wing-half after beginning his career with Wolverhampton Wanderers. Unable to gain a regular first team place at Molineux, he moved to Oldham Athletic. At Boundary Park he caught the eye of a number of talent spotters by his tenacity and ability and a year later joined Preston North End.

His non-stop endeavour soon earned him popularity with the Deepdale fans but after 62 league appearances he joined neighbours Blackburn Rovers. After a spell with Hull City he played for Sheffield Wednesday and scored the goal which kept the Owls in the Second Division against Bolton in April 1974. He toured New Zealand with an FA XI in 1969 and made a total of 359 league appearances for his six clubs.

After working as a coach at Roker Park, Ken Knighton became manager in June 1979 and took the club to runners-up spot in the Second Division in 1979-80. As a manager, the Barnsley-born Knighton had a reputation for being a strict disciplinarian and occasionally alienated his players with this approach. In April 1981 with the club struggling in the lower reaches of the First Division, Knighton was relieved of his duties. He later managed Orient but the Brisbane Road club were relegated at the end of his first season in charge and he was dismissed when they struggled again the following season.

Knighton then had spells managing non-League Dagenham Town and Trowbridge Town before leaving the game.

Sunderland's full league record under Ken Knighton is:

P	W	D	L	F	A
80	33	19	28	115	91

KUBICKI, DARIUS

Polish international full-back Darius Kubicki, who has won 49 caps for his country, began his career with Legia Warsaw before joining Aston Villa for £200,000 in the summer of 1991. Unable to settle at Villa Park, he had made just 34 first team appearances when he signed for Sunderland for a fee of £100,000 in March 1994.

After making his debut in a 2-0 home win over Notts County he played in the remaining 15 games of the 1993-94 season and was ever-present the following two campaigns in making 112 consecutive league appearances from his debut. Having won a Cup winners' medal in his homeland, he was able to add a First Division Championship medal to his collection in 1995-96, a season in which he was also honoured by his fellow professionals when he was selected for the PFA XI.

Though he lost his first team place to Gareth Hall in 1996-97, he fought his way back into the reckoning and played a number of games at left-back. He went on to appear in 150 first team games for the

Wearsiders before joining Wolverhampton Wanderers on a free transfer in the summer of 1997.

Things did not work out for him at Molineux and in March 1998 he was loaned out to Tranmere Rovers before being released at the end of the season.

KYLE, BOB

Sunderland's longest-serving manager, Bob Kyle was the secretary of the Irish League club Distillery in his native Belfast from the summer of 1897 until he joined Sunderland as secretary-manager in August 1905.

During his 23 years with the club, the Wearsiders not only won the League Championship in 1912-13 and finished runners-up in 1922-23 but ended a campaign in third place in no less than five seasons. In the first of these seasons in which the club finished third, 1908-09, the Wearsiders beat Newcastle United who ended the campaign as League Champions, 9-1 at St James' Park! Kyle spent large sums of money trying to find a winning formula, bringing players of the calibre of Charlie Thomson, Jackie Mordue and the legendary Charlie Buchan to Roker Park.

The 1912-13 season started badly for the Wearsiders with only two points from the first seven games but after Kyle had strengthened the defence by signing Joe Butler and Charlie Gladwin and Buchan had scored five goals in a 7-0 defeat of Liverpool, they never looked back. The Reds went on to win the League Championship, four points ahead of the nearest rivals Aston Villa. Though the club had never been too successful in the FA Cup, they reached the final in 1912-13 but missed out on the double when they lost 1-0 to Aston Villa. After the First World War, Kyle had to rebuild the club and one of the players he brought in was Warney Cresswell from South Shields who went on to become one of the club's great players.

In 1922-23, Kyle led Sunderland to the runners-up spot in the First Division, six points behind champions Liverpool. The club's chance of winning the title went with a series of poor results in April. Kyle also produced another great find for the club in Dave Halliday who scored 42 goals in his first season with the club. At the end of the 1927-28 season, in which the club had struggled to avoid relegation, Kyle resigned his post as Sunderland manager.

Sunderland's full league record under Bob Kyle is:

P	W	D	L	F	A
758	345	141	272	1367	1157

L

LARGEST CROWD

It was on 8 March 1933 that Roker Park housed its largest crowd. The occasion was the FA Cup sixth round replay against Derby County. A staggering crowd of 75,118 saw Sunderland lose 1-0 after the first match had produced an eight-goal thriller.

LATE FINISHES

Sunderland's final match of the season against Brentford at Roker Park on 24 May 1947 is the latest date for the finish of any Wearsiders' season. During the Second World War the 1941-42 League War Cup competition continued up until the end of May. Thus, Sunderland's last competitive match in that campaign was the second leg of the final against Wolverhampton Wanderers at Molineux on 30 May 1942, which the home side won 4-1, after drawing the first leg at Roker Park 2-2.

LAWTHER, IAN

Ian Lawther was playing with Crusaders when he was spotted by Sunderland for whom he signed in March 1958. He had to wait until August 1959 before making his first team debut for the Wearsiders in a 3-0 defeat at Aston Villa. However, he soon came to prominence and over the next two seasons was the club's top scorer. In 1959-60 he netted 18 goals in 40 games including a hat-trick in a 4-0 home win over Swansea, whilst in 1960-61 he found the net 26 times in 43 outings including scoring his second hat-trick for the club in a 7-1 defeat of Luton Town. Whilst at Roker Park he won two of his four international caps, the first against Wales in 1960.

In July 1961 he was transferred to Blackburn Rovers and scored 21 goals in 59 league appearances before leaving for Scunthorpe United where he had an almost identical record. In November 1964, Lawther became the only player to sign for a club in the House of Commons when he joined Brentford. Lawther spent four seasons at Griffin Park, scoring 43 goals in 139 appearances.

In August 1968 he moved to Halifax Town and in his first season, helped the Yorkshire club to their first promotion. Lawther joined his last league club, Stockport County in the summer of 1971 and was joint-top scorer in his first two seasons with the Edgeley Park club before being converted to a centre-half. The popular Irishman ended his career after scoring 178 league goals in 598 appearances for his six Football League clubs.

LEADING GOALSCORERS
Sunderland have provided the Football League's divisional leading goalscorer on eight occasions:

1891-92	Johnny Campbell	Division One	32 goals
1892-93	Johnny Campbell	Division One	31 goals
1894-95	Johnny Campbell	Division One	22 goals
1911-12	George Holley *	Division One	25 goals
1922-23	Charlie Buchan	Division One	30 goals
1928-29	Dave Halliday	Division One	43 goals
1949-50	Dickie Davis	Division One	26 goals
1997-98	Kevin Phillips **	Division One	29 goals

* shared with Harry Hampton (Aston Villa) and David McLean (Sheffield Wednesday)
** shared with Pierre Van Hooijdonk (Nottingham Forest)

LEAGUE GOALS - CAREER HIGHEST
Charlie Buchan holds the Sunderland record for the most league goals with a career total of 209 goals between 1910-11 and 1924-25.

LEAGUE GOALS - LEAST CONCEDED
During the 1998-99 season, Sunderland conceded just 28 goals in 46 First

Division games as they ended the season as Champions, 18 points clear of runners-up Bradford City.

LEAGUE GOALS - MOST INDIVIDUAL
Dave Halliday holds the Sunderland record for the most league goals in a season with 43 scored in 1928-29 when the club finished fourth in Division One.

LEAGUE GOALS - MOST SCORED
Sunderland's highest goals tally in the Football League was during the First Division Championship-winning season of 1935-36 when they scored 109 goals.

LEAGUE VICTORY - HIGHEST
Sunderland's best league victory is the 9-1 win over Newcastle United at St James' Park on 5 December 1908. Billy Hogg and George Holley both hit hat-tricks, Arthur Bridgett scored two and Jackie Mordue scored one in front of a stunned 60,000 crowd. Remarkably, Sunderland completed the double over the Magpies who ended the season as the League Champions!

LEE, BOB
Bob Lee began his Football League career with his local club Leicester City and in four seasons of First Division football with the Filberts scored 17 goals in 65 league games. After a loan spell with Doncaster Rovers, he joined Sunderland for a fee of £200,000 in September 1976.

He made his debut for the Wearsiders in a 1-0 home defeat by Everton on 2 October 1976 and went on to score 13 goals in 34 league appearances including a hat-trick in a 6-1 home win over West Bromwich Albion.

At the end of that season, Sunderland were relegated and Lee spent the next two seasons at Roker Park playing Second Division football. He had scored 33 goals in 123 League and Cup games when he was transferred to Bristol Rovers for £70,000 in August 1980.

After just one season with the Eastville club, he was on the move again, this time to Carlisle United, where he netted 12 goals in 55 league games for the Cumbrian side. He then had a spell playing in Hong Kong before returning to the north-east to see out his league career with Darlington.

LOW, HARRY

One of the club's earliest utility players, Harry Low joined Sunderland from Aberdeen in the summer of 1907 and made his debut at centre-half in a 5-2 home defeat by Manchester City on the opening day of the 1907-08 season. He was moved to inside-right for the next game and scored the winning goal in a 4-3 victory over Notts County. He missed very few games over the next eight seasons and was ever-present in 1912-13 when the club won the League Championship and appeared in all the Wearsiders' cup games as they reached the final against Aston Villa. His best season for the club in terms of goals scored was 1909-10 when he netted 15 in 27 games, playing predominantly at centre-forward. The following season he scored his only hat-trick for the club in a 3-1 home win over Middlesbrough and went on to score 38 goals in 228 League and Cup games before retiring in the summer of 1919 after making five appearances in the Victory League.

LOWEST

The lowest number of goals scored by Sunderland in a single league season is 30 in 1969-70 when the club finished 21st in the First Division and were relegated. The club's lowest points record in the League occurred in seasons 1890-91 and 1896-97 when the Wearsiders gained just 23 points.

M

MACKIE, ALEX

An administrator who never played professional football, Alex Mackie was associated with a number of Scottish clubs before becoming Sunderland's third manager in the summer of 1899.

Despite starting the 1899-1900 season well, with eight wins and a draw out of their first eleven games, the Wearsiders' form slipped somewhat and they had to settle for third place behind champions Aston Villa and runners-up Sheffield United. In 1900-01 the club only suffered six defeats in the whole of the season and finished as runners-up to Liverpool. In 1901-02, Sunderland won the League Championship with unspectacular football, only conceding 35 goals. The following season they were third again just a point behind champions Sheffield Wednesday.

In 1903, the FA investigated the club's books after Andy McCombie claimed that Sunderland had paid him £100 to start a business. The club said that the payment had been a loan but when the books were examined, irregularities were found. Alex Mackie was banned for three months but when he did return to the club, he sold Alf Common to Middlesbrough for £1,000 the first four-figure transfer fee in the history of the game. Soon afterwards, Mackie followed Common to Ayresome Park as Middlesbrough's manager.

He signed the legendary Steve Bloomer in March 1906 but once again accusations began to fly and again the FA were called in to look into the matter. Illegal payments had again been made to players and books had not been kept properly. Suspended for a second time, the disillusioned Mackie left the game to run a pub in Middlesbrough.

Sunderland's full league record under Alex Mackie is:

P	W	D	L	F	A
204	102	44	58	331	225

MALONE, DICK

Full-back Dick Malone joined Sunderland from Ayr United for a fee of £30,000 in October 1970 and played his first game in the red and white stripes of the Wearsiders in a 1-0 home win over Bristol City. Though he only scored two goals during his seven seasons at Roker Park, his first on 9 April 1971 was the only goal of the game against Orient and brought the club two valuable points. From 1971-72, Malone missed just five games in five seasons football, being ever-present in 1973-74 and

Dick Malone

1974-75 and playing in 98 consecutive league games.

He was a member of the Sunderland side that won the FA Cup Final in 1973 and won a Second Division Championship medal in 1975-76. At the end of the club's first season back in the top flight, Malone, who had appeared in 277 League and Cup games for the club was allowed to leave and joined Hartlepool United on a free transfer. He later ended his career with Blackpool, playing in 53 League and Cup games for the Bloomfield Road club.

MANAGERS

This is the complete list of Sunderland's full-time managers with the inclusive dates during which they held office:

Tom Watson	1890-1896	Jimmy Adamson	1976-1978
Robert Campbell	1896-1899	Billy Elliott	1978-1979
Alex Mackie	1899-1905	Ken Knighton	1979-1981
Bob Kyle	1905-1928	Alan Durban	1981-1984
Johnny Cochrane	1928-1939	Len Ashurst	1984-1985
Bill Murray	1939-1957	Lawrie McMenemy	1985-1987
Alan Brown	1957-1964	Denis Smith	1987-1991
George Hardwick	1964-1965	Malcolm Crosby	1991-1993
Ian McColl	1965-1968	Terry Butcher	1993
Alan Brown	1968-1972	Mick Buxton	1993-1995
Bob Stokoe	1972-1976	Peter Reid	1995-

MAPSON, JOHNNY

Birkenhead-born goalkeeper Johnny Mapson began his career with non-League Guildford City before joining Reading in April 1935.

He went on to make just two league appearances for the then Elm Park club before signing for Liverpool in March 1936. The agile 'keeper made his debut for the Wearsiders in a 5-0 home win over Portsmouth and played in the last seven games of the club's League Championship-winning season. He missed just one league game the following season and appeared in all of the club's matches during their run to the FA Cup Final where they beat Preston North End 3-1.

During the war, he played international football for England, and on his return to Roker Park for the first peacetime season of league football since the hostilities in 1946-47, he was an ever-present. He went on to appear in 385 League and Cup games for Sunderland, playing the last of them in a 3-3 draw against Manchester City in March 1953, some 17 years after joining the club.

MARATHON MATCHES

Sunderland have been involved in a number of cup games that have gone to three matches. These were Newcastle United (FA Cup fourth round 1912-13); Stoke City (FA Cup fourth round 1931-32); Wolverhampton Wanderers (FA Cup sixth round 1936-37); Blackburn Rovers (FA Cup fifth round 1938-39); Manchester United (FA Cup sixth round 1963-64); Leeds United (FA Cup fifth round 1966-67); Cardiff City (FA Cup fourth round 1971-72); Derby County (League Cup second round 1973-74) and Manchester United (League Cup third round 1976-77).

The FA Cup tie against Manchester United in 1963-64 attracted 163,379 spectators over the three matches.

MARKSMEN - LEAGUE

Sunderland's top league goalscorer is Charlie Buchan who struck 209 league goals during his eleven seasons at Roker Park. Only nine players have hit more than 100 league goals for the club.

1.	Charlie Buchan	209
2.	Bob Gurney	205
3.	Dave Halliday	153
4.	George Holley	145
5.	Johnny Campbell	133
6.	Raich Carter	121
7.	Arthur Bridgett	111
8.	Jimmy Millar	106
9.	Patsy Gallacher	101
10.	Len Shackleton	98
11.	Gary Rowell	84
12.	Billy Hogg	83
13.	Jackie Mordue	73
14.	Dickie Davis	72
15.	Billy Hughes	71
16.	Bobby Marshall	68
17.	Charlie Fleming	62
18.	Bryan Robson	60
19.	George Mulhall	55
20.	Bobby Kerr	53

MARKSMEN - OVERALL

Eleven players have hit over a century of goals for Sunderland. The club's top marksman is Bob Gurney. The Century Club consists of:

1.	Bob Gurney	228
2.	Charlie Buchan	224
3.	Dave Halliday	162
4.	George Holley	154
5.	Johnny Campbell	150
6.	Raich Carter	130
7.	Jimmy Millar	123
8.	Arthur Bridgett	119
9.	Patsy Gallacher	108
10.	Gary Rowell	101
	Len Shackleton	101

MARSHALL, BOBBY

Bobby Marshall played his early football with his home-town team Hucknall Olympics before joining Sunderland in May 1920. He played his first game for the north-east club at Bradford City in October of that year, scoring in a 2-2 draw.

After scoring 20 League and Cup goals in 1924-25 he repeated the feat in 1926-27 when his total included hat-tricks in the defeats of Arsenal (Home 5-1) and Bolton Wanderers (Home 6-2). He had scored 73 goals in 205 games for Sunderland when in March 1928 he left the Roker Park club to sign for Manchester City.

With the Maine Road club, Marshall appeared in consecutive FA Cup Finals, with a winners' medal in 1934, and was a member of the City side that won the League Championship for the first time in 1937-38. Marshall made 355 League and Cup appearances for City before transferring to Stockport County in March 1939. He later managed the Edgeley Park club as well as Chesterfield.

MARTIN, HARRY

Outside-left Harry Martin made his Sunderland debut at Anfield on 5 April 1912, scoring the Wearsiders' goal in a 2-1 defeat. He also netted on his home debut the following day as the other Merseyside club Everton were beaten 4-0. The following season, he was an ever-present as Sunderland won the League Championship, scoring five goals in 38 games. In 1914 he was capped by England in the match against Northern Ireland at Middlesbrough but was on the losing side as England crashed 3-0.

During the First World War, the Selston-born player 'guested' for Nottingham Forest and was a member of the side that won the Victory Shield in 1919. He returned to Roker Park after the hostilities, but in May 1922 after scoring 24 goals in 231 League and Cup games for the north-east club he joined Forest on a permanent basis.

He made his debut for the City Ground club in the opening game of the 1922-23 season as Forest beat his former club 1-0. The club's regular penalty taker during his time with Forest, he scored 13 goals in 114 games before joining Rochdale at the end of the 1924-25 season. He became their trainer in 1929 before managing Mansfield Town from 1933 to 1935. In 1936 he joined Swindon Town as trainer and remained on the staff of the County Ground club until the early 1950s.

MARTIN, NEIL

Neil Martin served an apprenticeship as a mining engineer whilst at Alloa before later playing for Queen of the South and Hibernian. He became a prolific goalscorer at Easter Road, scoring 40 goals in 1964-65. He had scored 78 goals in Scottish football when in October 1965, Sunderland manager Ian McColl paid Hibernian £50,000 for his services.

He scored on his debut in a 3-1 defeat at Sheffield Wednesday and ended the 1965-66 campaign with eight goals in 24 league games. In 1966-67, Martin scored 26 League and Cup goals in 48 games including hat-tricks against Blackpool in the league (Home 4-0) and Peterborough United in the FA Cup (Home 7-1). He went on to score 46 goals in 100 League and Cup appearances before joining Coventry City in February 1968.

Though he only played in the last 15 games of the season, he was the club's joint-top scorer with eight goals including a hat-trick against Sheffield Wednesday which helped the Sky Blues avoid the drop to the Second Division. His form earned him a recall to the Scottish national squad but after four seasons at Highfield Road in which he scored 45 goals in 122 games he was surprisingly allowed to join Nottingham Forest. Injuries hampered his progress at the City Ground and he moved on to have spells with both Brighton and Crystal Palace.

He was joint-manager with Alan Buckley at Walsall for a while, having previously been the youth team coach but in his only season in charge, the Saddlers just missed relegation by one place on goal difference.

MATCH OF THE DAY

Sunderland's first appearance on BBC's TV's 'Match of the Day' was on 11 March 1967 when they drew 1-1 at home to Leeds United in a fifth round FA Cup tie. The Wearsiders' scorer that day was Neil Martin in a match watched by a crowd of 55,763.

McALLISTER, ALEX

Scottish international Alex 'Sandy' McAllister joined Sunderland from Kilmarnock in December 1896 and made his first team debut in a 4-1 home win over Stoke. He was an ever-present in three of his seven seasons with the club and missed very few matches in the others. When he scored his first goal for the club in a 1-1 draw at Preston North End on 5 January 1901, the dependable defensive centre-half was presented with a piano and a gold watch by the fans to mark his achievement. Though not noted for his goalscoring, two of the five goals he scored for the Wearsiders came in the 3-1 home win over Bury on St Valentine's Day 1903.

McAllister had appeared in 225 League and Cup games for Sunderland when he left Roker Park to join Derby County in the summer of 1904.

McCOIST, ALLY

Ally McCoist began his career with St Johnstone before joining Sunderland for a fee of £400,000 in the summer of 1981. This was a huge amount at the time for such a young player. He made his full debut in a 1-1 draw at Arsenal on 12 September 1981 but his time at Roker Park was not successful and in June 1983 after scoring just nine goals in 74 League and Cup outings, he signed for Glasgow Rangers for £185,000.

When Rangers' new manager Jock Wallace replaced John Greig, he suggested to McCoist that a transfer back to Sunderland could be arranged. He decided to stay and fight for a place and midway through the 1984-85 season he became a regular, and in April 1986 won his first cap for Scotland.

He was the club's top scorer for six consecutive seasons from 1983-84 and then in 1991-92, he netted 41 goals including a personal career total of 200 Scottish League goals. This performance brought McCoist the European award of the 'Golden Boot'. He was voted 'Player of the Year' by the Scottish Football Writers' Association and by the Scottish players themselves. He then did the impossible by winning the award again the following season, with 34 goals in 34 league games, the only player to win the European Golden Boot award in consecutive years.

At the end of the 1997-98 season, McCoist who had scored 250 goals for the Ibrox club, left to join Kilmarnock.

Ally McCoist

McCOLL, IAN

Ian McColl developed into one of Scotland's finest right-halves and as well as representing the Scottish League on seven occasions, he also won 14 full caps for his country. An excellent passer of the ball, he made well over 400 first team appearances for Rangers, with whom he won six Scottish League Championship medals, five Scottish Cup winners' medals and two Scottish League Cup winners' medals.

On his retirement from the playing side of the game, he was appointed manager of the Scottish national side, though he did not have sole charge of the team. The Scottish FA picked the side and also had a great say in tactics. Within a month of leaving his post as the national team manager, he was appointed manager of Sunderland.

He spent £340,000 on nine new players including Scottish internationals Jim Baxter (£75,000 from Rangers) and Neil Martin (£80,000 from Hibernian) but the blend was still missing and the club finished 19th, just three points clear of Second Division football. There was a slight improvement the following season and again in 1967-68, but during this campaign the Reds lost 1-0 at home to Norwich City in an FA Cup third round replay and this hastened the end of McColl's reign as Sunderland manager.

Sunderland's full league record under Ian McColl is:

P	W	D	L	F	A
126	41	27	58	160	205

McCOMBIE, ANDREW

Full-back Andrew McCombie joined Sunderland from Inverness Thistle in December 1898 but did not make his first team debut until 18 February 1899 when he starred in a 1-0 win at Sheffield Wednesday. The following season he was an ever-present as the club finished third in Division One in what was Alex Mackie's first season as Sunderland manager. In fact, McCombie missed very few matches over the next five seasons for Sunderland, his outstanding form winning him two full caps in 1903 when he played against England and Wales. He had appeared in 164 games for the Wearsiders when he moved to Newcastle United for a staggering £700, a record at the time.

McCombie left Roker Park in controversial circumstances, his departure being in connection with a payment of £100. McCombie said that the £100 was a gift from the Sunderland directors, who in turn, said the £100 was a loan! The differing views led to a court case and an FA Inquiry which resulted in Alex Mackie the Sunderland manager being suspended for three months for making illegal payments.

He won League and Cup medals at St James' Park and after hanging up his boots after playing in 131 games he remained with the Magpies until 1950 as a member of the club's backroom staff.

McDOUGALL, JOCK

The older brother of Jimmy McDougall who played for Partick Thistle, Liverpool and Scotland, Jock McDougall worked as a marine engineer on Clydeside and played for Kilmacolm Amateurs, then Port Glasgow Juniors before signing for Airdrie in November 1921. He won a full cap against Northern Ireland in 1926, represented the Scottish League twice and picked up a Scottish Cup winners' medal in 1924.

In May 1929 he joined Sunderland for a fee of £4,500 and was made club captain. He played his first game for the Wearsiders in a 5-2 home win over Manchester City on 7 September 1929 and over the next five seasons, missed very few games. He went on to play in 184 League and Cup games for Sunderland before Leeds United beat Plymouth Argyle to sign the 33-year-old defender for £6,000. He skippered Leeds United for the next three seasons, appearing in 59 games before retiring.

McINROY, ALBERT

Born at Walton-le-Dale near Preston, Albert McInroy was an outside-left with St Thomas High School in Preston. After leaving school and getting a job as a packer at the Preston Co-operative Society, he played in goal for local sides Upper Walton and Coppull Central. After failing to make the grade with Preston North End, he joined Leyland Motors in November 1922. After some impressive performances, he signed for Sunderland in May 1923 and was given his Football League debut on 29 September 1923 as the Wearsiders beat Manchester City 5-2. He quickly established himself as the club's first-choice 'keeper and over the next six seasons, played in 227 League and Cup games. His form was such during this period that he won a full England cap in October 1926 against Northern Ireland at Anfield. The game ended all-square at 3-3 but McInroy was never selected again.

In October 1929 he was transferred to Newcastle United for £2,750 and won an FA Cup winners' medal in 1932. He returned to Roker Park in the summer of 1934 but failed to oust both Middleton and Thorpe and joined Leeds in June 1935. He made 67 appearances for the Elland Road club, turning in some highly agile performances before leaving to play with Gateshead. He later kept goal for Stockton before seeing out his career with a number of minor clubs in the north-east.

McMENEMY, LAWRIE

Lawrie McMenemy failed to make the grade as a player with Newcastle United and joined his local club Gateshead, but in 1961, an injury ended his career and he became trainer-coach at the club for the next three years. In 1964 he was appointed manager of Bishop Auckland and transformed them into Northern Premier League champions.

After two years as coach at Sheffield Wednesday he was appointed manager of Doncaster Rovers and in his first season in charge took them to the championship of the Fourth Division. However, when the Belle Vue club were relegated in 1971, McMenemy was sacked. A week later he was appointed manager of Grimsby Town and again at the end of his first season in charge, they won the Fourth Division championship.

In the summer of 1973 he accepted an offer to become Ted Bates' assistant-manager at The Dell but six months later he was appointed the club's full-time manager. At the end of that season the Saints were relegated and McMenemy came in for a lot of criticism when they did not bounce straight back but he did take the club to a shock FA Cup Final victory over Manchester United in 1976.

In 1977-78 the Saints won promotion to the First Division and a year later reached the League Cup Final where they lost to Nottingham Forest. In 1983-84 the Saints enjoyed their best-ever season in the First Division when they finished runners-up.

In June 1985 McMenemy moved to Sunderland but he had a tough time at Roker Park with the club just avoiding relegation to the Third Division in his first season in charge. The following season the club's performances were even worse and in April 1987, he was sacked. After three years out of the game, McMenemy returned as assistant-manager to England boss Graham Taylor but is now manager of Northern Ireland.

Sunderland's full league record under Lawrie McMenemy is:

P	W	D	L	F	A
77	23	21	33	86	109

McNAB, JIMMY

Jimmy McNab began his footballing career with his home-town team Denny Juniors. Recruited by Sunderland when he was 15, on the strength of a Scottish cap and promise shown with Kilsyth Rangers, he went on to make his debut for the Roker Park club in a 2-0 home defeat by Ipswich Town in September 1958. Over the next eight seasons, McNab missed very few games and was ever-present in 1961-62. In 1963-64 he played a major role in the Wearsiders winning promotion to the First Division and from his position at wing-half, went on to score 18 goals in 324 first team games before signing for Preston North End in March 1967.

Strong in the tackle and a good distributor of the ball, he was a virtual ever-present in his seven seasons at Deepdale. After making 224 league appearances for the Lilywhites, he moved to Stockport County in the summer of 1974, where he made the last of his 539 Football League appearances.

Jimmy McNab

McPHAIL, JOHN

John McPhail began his career with his home-town club Dundee with a substitute appearance at Ibrox in April 1976 which Rangers won 3-0. He went on to make 84 first team appearances for the Dens Park club before leaving to join Sheffield United.

He bolstered a leaky Blades defence and after scoring United's goal in the televised derby with Sheffield Wednesday which finished 1-1, had the pleasure of netting the only goal of the Yorkshire club's Anglo-Scottish tie against his former club at Dens Park. McPhail played in 160 first team games for Sheffield United before joining York City on a permanent basis following an earlier loan spell.

In his first full season at Bootham Crescent, he helped the club win the

Fourth Division title with 101 points, playing in every game and scoring ten league goals. He had appeared in 157 games for York City when in 1986 he moved to Bristol City. After just one season at Ashton Gate, Denis Smith, his boss at York, brought him to Roker Park for a fee of £23,000.

McPhail made his Sunderland debut in a 1-0 win at Brentford on the opening day of the 1987-88 season, a campaign in which he was ever-present as the club won the Third Division championship. He also scored 16 league goals and was voted into third place by local sportswriters in the awards for the north-east Footballer of the Year. He went on to appear in 153 first team games for the Wearsiders before leaving the club in September 1990 and signing for Hartlepool United.

MELVILLE, ANDY

Swansea-born Andy Melville began his career with his home-town club and progressed from the youth training scheme to make his senior debut against Bristol City in November 1985. In his early days there was something of a problem in that his best position was not readily apparent. He was tried in most positions before settling into the back four. He won a permanent place in the Swansea side in 1986-87 and helped the Swans win promotion the following season.

He was appointed Swansea captain at the age of 20 but in July 1990 after playing in 213 games for the Vetch Field club, he joined Oxford United for £275,000 plus a percentage of any future transfer fee. In three seasons at the Manor Ground he appeared in 159 games before being transferred to Sunderland in the summer of 1993.

The Welsh international who won 32 caps for his country, made a disastrous Sunderland debut in a 5-0 defeat at Derby County on the opening day of the 1993-94 season. His first two seasons at Roker Park were spent in relegation battles but in 1995-96 Melville played in 40 league games as the Wearsiders won the First Division championship.

Powerful in the air and always dangerous from set pieces from where he has scored some important goals, he acquitted himself well in the Premiership. Sadly, a broken nose ruled him out of the last seven games of the season when his experience could have helped the club in their attempt to avoid the drop.

In 1997-98 an injury ended his virtual monopoly of a back-four place and when he recovered he was loaned out to Bradford City. One of the club's most experienced players, Melville continues to be part of the Wearsider's success.

MILLAR, JIMMY

Jimmy Millar joined the Wearsiders from Annbank in August 1890 and made his debut in the club's first game in the Football League, a 3-2 defeat at the hands of Burnley. That season he netted the first of 10 hat-tricks for the club in a 4-0 home win over Notts County. The following season of 1891-92 saw Millar net the first of three hat-tricks against Wolverhampton Wanderers in a 7-2 victory and then find the net four times as Derby County were beaten 7-1 which Sunderland went on to win the League Championship for the first time. Millar continued his prolific goalscoring in 1892-93, scoring 16 goals in 23 games including his fourth hat-trick for the club in a 6-0 FA Cup victory over Royal Arsenal and picking up another League Championship medal. His best season in terms of goals scored was 1893-94 when, included in his total of 20 goals in 27 games was another hat-trick against Wolves in a 6-0 win.

The Scotsman won his third League Championship medal in 1894-95 but it was in the FA Cup that he hit the headlines, netting five of the club's goals in an 11-1 FA Cup win over non-League Fairfield. After scoring another hat-trick in a 7-1 win over West Bromwich Albion the following season, Millar returned to his native Scotland to sign for Glasgow Rangers.

Whilst with the Ibrox club Millar won three full caps for Scotland and in his first match scored the winning goal as the Scots beat England 2-1.

He returned to Sunderland for the start of the 1900-01 season, during the course of which he scored his third hat-trick against Wolves in a 7-2 home win. He won his fourth League Championship medal in 1901-02 when, included in his total of eight league goals, were hat-tricks against Nottingham Forest (Home 4-0) and Bury (Home 3-0).

He had scored 123 goals in 260 games during his two spells with the club leaving Roker Park in the summer of 1904 to join West Bromwich Albion.

MONTGOMERY, JIM

Sunderland-born goalkeeper Jim Montgomery joined his home-town club on leaving school in 1958 and turned professional at Roker Park in October 1960. He made his league debut in a 2-1 home win over Derby County on 24 February 1962 and went on to become a permanent fixture for the next 16 seasons, though he missed much of the 1964-65 season with a hand injury. He was ever-present in five seasons including 1963-64 when the club won promotion to the First Division as runners-up to Leeds United. He won an FA Cup winners' medal in 1973 when his never-to-be-forgotten double save thwarted Leeds United. There is no doubt that Jim

Montgomery was one of the best goalkeepers in the Football League during the 1960s and early 1970s, and but for the presence of Gordon Banks, he may well have added a full England cap to his England Youth and Under-23 honours.

Montgomery who went on to appear in a club record total of 623 first team appearances for the Wearsiders joined Birmingham City on a free transfer in February 1977 after a loan spell at Southampton.

He made 73 appearances for the St Andrews club before signing for Nottingham Forest as cover for Peter Shilton. After a short spell as temporary coach at Birmingham he returned home to Sunderland to become senior coach at Roker Park.

One of the greatest 'keepers in the club's history, he was 37 when the Wearsiders resigned him as a non-contract reserve goalkeeper.

Jim Montgomery

MORDUE, JACKIE

Jackie Mordue began his career in junior football with Sacriston and Spennymoor United before playing for Barnsley Town. Woolwich Arsenal paid the Yorkshire club £450 for his services in April 1907, the tricky forward linking up with his brother-in-law Jimmy Ashcroft. With Mordue being one of Arsenal's best assets, it came as no surprise when a £750 offer from Sunderland was accepted in May 1908.

He made his debut for the Wearsiders in a 3-0 win at Middlesbrough on 9 September 1908 and went on to have a glittering eight season career at Roker Park, playing in 299 League and Cup games and scoring 83 goals. His best season in terms of goals scored was 1912-13 when his 19 strikes in 47 games helped the club win the League Championship and to a losing appearance in the FA Cup Final against Aston Villa. He won the first of his two England caps against Ireland in 1911-12 and also represented the Football League on three occasions.

His best years were probably lost to the First World War, however he played for a further season at Sunderland before being transferred to Middlesbrough in May 1920. He spent two seasons at Ayresome Park before finishing his career with Hartlepool United in 1922-23 and as player-manager of Durham City in 1923-24. After Durham had beat local rivals Darlington 3-2 in February 1924, Mordue was sacked as he was considered 'unsuitable for the post' by the club's directors.

MOST MATCHES
Sunderland played their most number of matches, 59 in season 1989-90. This comprised 46 league games, one FA Cup game, eight League Cup games, one Zenith Data Systems Cup game and three play-off games.

MULHALL, GEORGE
An exciting left-winger with an eye for goal, George Mulhall came from a footballing family, his two brothers playing for Falkirk and Albion Rovers. Joining Aberdeen in 1953, he scored 42 goals in 150 games for the Pittodrie club and won a Scottish League Cup winners' medal in 1959 before leaving to join Sunderland in September 1962.

His first game in Sunderland colours came in a 4-2 defeat at Rotherham United but his form was so good, that he won his second full cap for Scotland when he played against Northern Ireland, having won his first whilst with Aberdeen. In 1963-64 when Sunderland won promotion to the First Division, Mulhall was an ever-present, scoring eight goals in 42 games including three in the opening two games of the season. He went on to score 66 goals in 291 League and Cup games before leaving to play for Cape Town in South Africa, where he won League and Cup medals.

In October 1971 he joined Halifax Town as player-coach before being appointed manager eight months later. He then joined Bolton Wanderers as assistant to Ian Greaves before leaving to become manager at Bradford City in 1978. He returned to Bolton for a second spell with the club, being appointed manager in the summer of 1981. Though he saved the Trotters from relegation, there was conflict between Mulhall and the Board over the sale of Paul Jones, and in June 1982 he left the club.

Mulhall then worked as assistant to Frank Worthington at Tranmere before becoming chief scout, youth development officer and assistant-manager of Huddersfield Town. He is now in his second spell as manager of Halifax Town.

MURRAY, BILL

Bill Murray was studying engineering with a view to working with a shipping firm in Shanghai when he was approached by a number of clubs, all wishing him to play football for them. He chose Cowdenbeath, so that he could continue with his studies, and over the next couple of years, developed into a stylish right-back. He captained the Central Park club into the Scottish First Division in 1924 and had made 111 appearances for them before joining Sunderland along with David Wright in a deal worth £8,000.

After missing the opening game of the 1927-28 season, Murray made his debut in a 4-2 win at West Ham United and went on to appear in 56 consecutive matches, before following an injury, he lost his place to Oakley. It wasn't too long before he regained his place and, over the next nine seasons became a virtual ever-present. After helping the Wearsiders win the League Championship in 1935-36, Murray, who had played in 328 League and Cup games for Sunderland, moved back to Scotland to play for St Mirren.

He returned to Roker Park as the club's manager just before the outbreak of the Second World War and produced a very skilful side with plenty of personalities including the great Len Shackleton. The club's best position in Murray's 11 full seasons in charge was third in 1949-50, though he did take the club to two FA Cup semi-finals in 1955 and 1956.

Murray resigned his post as Sunderland manager after an illegal payment scandal at the club.

Sunderland's full league record under Bill Murray is:

P	W	D	L	F	A
462	165	129	168	746	795

N

NEUTRAL GROUNDS

Roker Park was used as early as 1899 for an England v Ireland international, a fixture that was again held at Sunderland's ground in 1920. The result of that first international, in which Sunderland's Philip Bach won his only cap, was 13-2 to England!

The last international match involving England to be played at Roker Park was the game against Wales in 1950, which the home side with Sunderland's Willie Watson in their ranks, won 4-2. The ground also staged four games in the 1966 World Cup including the quarter-final between USSR and Hungary. Roker Park was also the venue for the FA Amateur Finals of 1926 and 1939, and in 1955 staged the FA Cup semi-final replay between Newcastle United and York City.

Sunderland themselves of course have had to replay on a neutral ground a number of times.

Date	Opponents	Venue	Stage	Score
15.03.1937	Wolverhampton.W.	Hillsborough	Rd6 2R	4-0
18.02.1939	Blackburn Rovers	Hillsborough	Rd5 2R	0-1
09.03.1964	Manchester United	Leeds Road	Rd6 2R	1-5
20.03.1967	Leeds United	Boothferry Park	Rd5 2R	1-2
16.02.1972	Cardiff City	Maine Road	Rd4 2R	1-3

The club's semi-finals were also played on neutral grounds.

Date	Opponents	Venue	Score
28.02.1891	Notts County	Bramall Lane	3-3
11.03.1891	Notts County	Bramall Lane	0-2
27.02.1892	Aston Villa	Bramall Lane	1-4
16.03.1895	Aston Villa	Ewood Park	1-2
29.03.1913	Burnley	Bramall Lane	0-0
02.04.1913	Burnley	St Andrew's	3-2
14.03.1931	Birmingham City	Elland Road	0-2
10.04.1937	Millwall	Leeds Road	2-1
26.03.1938	Huddersfield Town	Ewood Park	1-3
26.03.1955	Manchester City	Villa Park	0-1
17.03.1956	Birmingham City	Hillsborough	0-3
07.04.1973	Arsenal	Hillsborough	2-1
05.04.1992	Norwich City	Hillsborough	1-0

The club's FA Cup and League Cup Final appearances at Crystal Palace and Wembley also qualify for inclusion.

NICKNAMES
Formerly known as the Rokerites, Sunderland's nickname is now usually the Wearsiders or the Reds.

Many players in the club's history have been known by their nicknames. They include:

Jimmy Watson	1900-1907	Daddy Long Legs
Charlie Fleming	1955-1959	Cannonball
Charlie Hurley	1957-1969	King Charlie

NON-LEAGUE
Non-League is the term used for clubs which are not members of the Football League. On 2 February 1895 the club established what is still their biggest ever victory in the competition when they beat Fairfield 11-1 with Jimmy Millar scoring five of the goals. Despite this success, in the years leading up to the First World War, the club had a poor FA Cup record and in 1898 lost 2-1 to Tottenham Hotspur of the Southern League and in 1910-11 lost 3-1 to Norwich City who were also then members of the Southern League.

However, the Wearsiders have a good record against non-League clubs in the FA Cup. The club's record since that defeat at the hands of the Canaries is:

Date	Opponents	Venue	Result
13.01.1912	Plymouth Argyle	Home	Won 3-1
03.02.1912	Crystal Palace	Away	Drew 0-0
07.02.1912	Crystal Palace	Home	Won 1-0
22.02.1913	Swindon Town	Home	Won 4-2
10.01.1914	Chatham	Home	Won 9-0
31.01.1914	Plymouth Argyle	Home	Won 2-1
09.01.1926	Boston	Home	Won 8-1
29.01.1949	Yeovil Town	Away	Lost 1-2 aet
12.02.1963	Gravesend	Away	Drew 1-1
18.02.1963	Gravesend	Home	Won 5-2

NORMAN, TONY

Welsh international goalkeeper Tony Norman began his career with Burnley but failed to make the grade at Turf Moor and joined Hull City for a fee of £30,000 in February 1980. At Boothferry Park he set a new club record of 226 consecutive league appearances and though receivership cast a shadow over the 'keeper's future with the Tigers, he stayed to help the club win promotion to the Third Division in 1982. He went on to appear in 442 League and Cup games for Hull City before joining Sunderland in December 1988, in a record £400,000 deal.

He made his debut on the last day of the year in a 4-0 home win over Portsmouth and played in the remaining 24 games of that season. In 1989-90 he helped the club into the Second Division play-offs where he kept clean sheets in both legs of the semi-final tie against Newcastle United. In the final against Swindon Town he was in magnificent form and though the Wearsiders lost 1-0 it would have been many more but for Norman.

The Deeside-born 'keeper did however play in the top flight. After investigations by the Inland Revenue and the Football League, Swindon were relegated and Sunderland were promoted in their place. He missed just one game in that 1990-91 campaign and though the club were relegated, he kept nine clean sheets in his 37 games. Norman played in 227 first team games for the Wearsiders before leaving to see out his league career with Huddersfield Town.

NORTHUMBERLAND AND DURHAM CUP

The Cup competition was open to any club playing Association Football in Northumberland and Durham and first took place during the 1880-81 season. After a bye in the first round, Sunderland met Burnopfield at the Blue House Field and were held to a 2-2 draw. In the replay, two goals from James Allan gave Sunderland victory. In the semi-final, Sunderland met Newcastle United at St James' Park but were well beaten 5-0.

In 1881-82 the Wearsiders crashed out of the competition at the first attempt, beaten 4-0 by Sedgefield in what was a very rough game. The following season Sunderland recorded their biggest victory to date when they beat Stanley Star 12-1 in the first round. They then defeated Haughton-le-Skerne 4-1 to reach the semi-final for a second time where they beat Derwent Rangers 1-0.

In the final, Sunderland lost 2-0 to Tyne. It was the nearest they came to winning the competition, as the following season it became known as The Durham Challenge Cup after the formation of the Durham Football Association.

O

OLDEST PLAYER

The oldest player to line up in a Sunderland team is Bryan 'Pop' Robson. He was 38 years 128 days old when he played his last game for the club, scoring one of the goals in a 2-0 win at Leicester City on 12 May 1984.

ORD, RICHARD

Left-sided centre-back Richard Ord made his Sunderland debut in the 7-0 home defeat of Southend United on 3 November 1987, and though he was a first team regular the following season, the next six seasons saw him in and out of the side. In fact, there was a time when Ord, who had a loan spell at York City in February 1990, could have left the Wearsiders. Thankfully he stayed, and in 1991 he was capped three times by England at Under-21 level.

Following Peter Reid's arrival as manager, he began to fulfil the promise he had shown in his early days with the club. He formed an outstanding central defensive partnership with Andy Melville and played in 41 league games in 1995-96 as the club won the First Division Championship. Excellent in the air and surprisingly skilful for such a big man, he enjoyed a testimonial at Sunderland in 1996 but not relegation from the Premiership after just one season. Ord was one of the club's most consistent performers in 1996-97 though he did pick up unnecessary red cards in two games. A back injury curtailed his number of appearances in 1997-98, though the popular defender was always ready when required. Richard Ord is currently Sunderland's longest-serving player and at the time of writing has appeared in over 300 games.

OVERSEAS PLAYERS

Probably the first overseas player to join the club was Claudio Marangoni, an Argentinian international who joined the Wearsiders from San Lorenzo in December 1979. He helped the club win promotion to the First Division but after just five appearances in the top flight he left to play in South American football with Huracan. Dutch winger Loek Ursem who had played his early football with AZ Alkmaar joined Sunderland on loan from Stoke City in March 1982 but after just six appearances as a substitute he returned to play for the Potters.

Thomas Hauser joined the north-east club from Basle Old Boys for a fee of £200,000 but spent most of his time at Roker Park on the bench, and in October 1992 left to play for Cambuur.

Darius Kubicki joined the Wearsiders from Aston Villa for a fee of £100,000 after a loan spell at the club. The Polish international full-back who won 49 caps for his country, appeared in 150 League and Cup games before joining Wolverhampton Wanderers.

Jan Eriksson arrived at Sunderland in January 1997 from Swedish club Helsingborg for a fee of £250,000. After an impressive debut at Aston Villa he was confined to the substitutes' bench as the Wearsiders slid towards relegation from the Premier League. Surprisingly he was allowed to leave the club after exactly one year and joined Tampa Bay Mutiny. The club have had other foreign players on their books such as Antonio Pacheco, Kim Heiselberg and Edwin Zoetebier, but they didn't make the first team.

Flamboyant French goalkeeper Lionel Perez joined the Wearsiders from Bordeaux in the summer of 1996 and became a cult figure with the fans. Sadly he left the club after two seasons to join arch rivals Newcastle United. Other players with foreign-sounding surnames include Reuben Agboola, Philip Bach, Daniele Dichio, Marco Gabbiadini, Roland Gregoire (who was the club's first coloured player) and Steve Hetzke - all born in the British Isles.

OWERS, GARY

Gary Owers played his first game in Sunderland's colours in a 1-0 win at Brentford on the opening day of the 1987-88 season. After that the competitive midfielder was a virtual ever-present for the next eight seasons, appearing in 320 first team games and scoring 27 goals.

At the end of his first season he had won a Third Division Championship-winners' medal and in 1989-90 helped the club win promotion to the First Division after Swindon Town, who had beaten the Wearsiders 1-0 in the play-off final were relegated to the Second Division after the discovery of financial irregularities at the County Ground club.

He left Roker Park in December 1994, joining Bristol City for a fee of £250,000. After suffering with injuries and a loss of form at Ashton Gate, he had a great 1996-97 season. An ever-present, he captained the Robins to the play-off semi-final where they lost to Brentford and scored many crucial goals throughout the campaign. Injuries hampered his progress in the 1998-99 season but he has still managed to appear in almost 200 games for the Ashton Gate club.

OWN GOALS

A number of Sunderland players have put through their own goals and including Charlie Hurley on his debut in a 7-0 defeat at the hands of Blackpool.

The most interesting story about own goals concerns full-back Charlie Gladwin. In the third round of the 1912-13 FA Cup competition, Sunderland were held to a goalless draw at Roker Park by Newcastle United. With only minutes remaining in the replay at St James' Park, the scores were level at 1-1 when Buchan put the Wearsiders ahead. But then a Colin Veitch free-kick for Newcastle was put into his own goal by Gladwin.

When extra-time failed to produce any more goals, the third game was arranged for St James' Park. Apparently,on his way home from the replay, Gladwin heard two men talking on the tram, speculating on how much the Sunderland full-back got paid for putting the ball through his own goal. His response was to hit the man so hard, he fell from the tram and was left sitting in the road! Sunderland won the third match 3-0 with goals from Mordue (2) and Holley.

P

PARKER, CHARLIE

Charlie Parker joined Stoke in January 1914 and soon established himself in the club's Southern League side. After football resumed following the First World War, Charlie Parker was instrumental in the Stoke line-up He was considered to be one of the best defenders in the country and many Stoke fans were disappointed when he was allowed to go to Sunderland in September 1920 when he was undoubtedly at the top of his career.

He played his first game for the Wearsiders in a 2-2 draw at Bradford City on 23 October 1920 and over the next nine seasons was a virtual ever-present in a Sunderland side that were runners-up in the First Division in 1922-23 and finished in third place on three occasions. Parker scored 12 goals in 256 League and Cup games for Sunderland before joining Carlisle United as player-coach and later finishing his footballing days at Blyth Spartans.

PASCOE, COLIN

Colin Pascoe joined Swansea City as a 16-year-old apprentice in 1981 when the Vetch Field club were in the First Division of the Football League. He made his debut against Brighton in March 1983 as a substitute when he replaced the injured John Mahoney. During his first season with the Swans, he represented the Welsh Youth side and in 1983-84 was chosen for the Welsh Under-21 side on four occasions. Two years after winning his Welsh Youth cap, he was selected for the Wales senior side against

Norway. Pascoe had played in 201 first team games for the Swans when Sunderland paid £70,000 for his services in March 1988.

After scoring the Wearsiders' goal in a 2-1 defeat at York City on his debut, Pascoe netted the winner against Chesterfield in a 3-2 win for Sunderland on his second appearance, his home debut. He also scored in his third game for the north-east club in a 4-1 win at Southend United.

He helped the Wearsiders reach the First Division via the play-offs, even though it was at the expense of Swindon Town who were found guilty of financial irregularities and relegated from the top flight. Pascoe went on to score 26 goals in 151 games before returning to Swansea after a loan spell with the Vetch Field club.

He took his total of goals for the Swans to 67 in 324 League and Cup games before being released by the club after suffering damage to his ankle ligaments.

PENALTIES

Missed penalties have cost Sunderland dearly! In 1949-50, Sunderland needed to win just one of their last three games against Middlesbrough, Manchester City or Huddersfield Town to win the League Championship. The Wearsiders lost all three games and saw the title go to Portsmouth on goal average above Wolverhampton Wanderers, with Sunderland third. Sunderland lost 2-1 to Manchester City whose German-born 'keeper Bert Trautmann saved a twice-taken penalty by Jack Stelling!

When Sunderland played Norwich City in the League Cup Final of 1985, the Wearsiders lost 1-0 with Clive Walker missing a second-half penalty.

In the play-off penalty shoot-out against Charlton Athletic, Michael Gray saw his spot-kick saved by Sasa Ilic and with it went the Wearsiders' chances of playing Premier League football in 1998-99.

PENALTY SHOOT-OUTS

The club have been involved in a number of penalty shoot-outs over the years. One which gave the club real satisfaction was the League Cup game against Newcastle United in 1979-80. A 2-2 home draw was followed by a 2-2 draw at St James' Park, necessitating a penalty shoot-out. Jim Pearson the Magpies' forward, was the only Newcastle player not to score, resulting in a 7-6 victory to Sunderland.

In the 1997-98 Wembley play-off final against Charlton Athletic, a penalty shoot-out was required after the game had ended 4-4 after extra-time.

Charlton 'keeper Sasa Ilic stopped Michael Gray's spot-kick, a save calculated to be worth at least £10 million to the London club who won promotion to the Premiership.

PEREZ, LIONEL

French goalkeeper Lionel Perez joined Sunderland from Bordeaux for a fee of £200,000 in the summer of 1996. Initially seen as cover for Tony Coton, he made his debut as a substitute when the club's Number One 'keeper suffered a serious injury in the 3-0 defeat at Southampton in October 1996. In his first full game for the club he kept a clean sheet in a 1-0 win over Aston Villa. Four games later he saved a penalty in the match at Everton which Sunderland won 3-1, and at the end of the season was voted the club's Player of the Year.

Despite the signing of Dutch 'keeper Edwin Zoetebier, the flamboyant Frenchman kept his place and proceeded to turn in a series of top-class performances, perhaps none better than in the club's 1-1 draw at Charlton Athletic on 15 March 1998 when he saved two certain goals in the dying seconds. He played in every league game in 1997-98 but after contractual problems forced the club to release him during the summer of 1998, he joined Newcastle United on a free transfer.

PHILLIPS, KEVIN

Kevin Phillips began his Football League career with Watford after being signed from non-League Baldock for £10,000 in December 1994. In fact, Phillips made his Watford debut in a 1-0 defeat at home to Sunderland for whom Craig Russell netted for the Wearsiders on 21 February 1995. He held his place for the rest of the season and was the club's joint top scorer with nine goals in 15 games. In 1995-96 he had scored 11 goals in 26 games when a broken foot brought his season to an early end. He was still troubled by the injury the following season but on his return, he netted the first hat-trick of his league career in a 3-0 win over Bristol City. In the summer of 1997, Phillips left Vicarage Road and joined Sunderland for a fee of £300,000 after having scored 25 goals in 63 games for the Hornets.

He scored on his debut in a 3-1 home win over Manchester City in what was the club's first league game at the Stadium of Light. Possessing tremendous pace, he formed a deadly partnership with Niall Quinn and earned a call-up to the England 'B' squad. During the course of the season, he scored in nine consecutive home league games and hit four goals in a 5-1 FA Cup win at Rotherham United. He ended a remarkable campaign with 35 goals, 29 of them in the league, to make him the First Division's leading marksman. His form in 1998-99 led to him winning international recognition for Kevin Keegan's England team.

PICKERING, NICK

After being spotted playing for North Shields Schoolboys, Nick Pickering signed for Sunderland as an apprentice. On turning professional in August 1981 he made his debut in a 3-3 draw at Ipswich Town on the opening day of the 1981-82 season. His consistent performances brought him to the attention of the international selectors, and in September 1982 he won the first of 15 Under-21 caps when he played for England against Denmark in Hvivodre.

The following summer whilst still only 19, he won his only full cap when he played in a 1-1 draw against Australia in Melbourne in June 1983. During the 1984-85 season, Pickering at the age of 21, captained Sunderland in

Nick Pickering

135

the League Cup Final clash with Norwich City at Wembley in March 1985. The Wearsiders lost 1-0 and just weeks later, they were relegated to the Second Division.

After making 211 first team appearances for Sunderland, he was transferred to Coventry City for £120,000 in January 1986, and at the end of his first full season with the Highfield Road club, was a member of the Sky Blues side that defeated Tottenham Hotspur 3-2 to win the 1987 FA Cup Final.

A fee of £250,000 took him to Derby County in the summer of 1988 but he was never an automatic choice at the Baseball Ground, and in October 1991 he signed for Darlington. He later ended his league career with Burnley whom he had joined in March 1993 for a fee of £15,000.

PITCH
The Stadium of Light pitch measures 115 yards by 75 yards. Roker Park measured 113 yards by 74 yards.

PLASTIC
Four league clubs replaced their normal grass playing pitches with artificial surfaces at one stage or another. Queen's Park Rangers were the first in 1981 but the Loftus Road plastic was discarded in 1988 in favour of a return to turf. Luton Town (1985) Oldham Athletic (1986) and Preston North End (1986) followed.

Sunderland never played on the Kenilworth Road plastic and failed to score a goal in two defeats at Queen's Park Rangers. Three visits to Oldham's Boundary Park plastic saw the Wearsiders draw two games and lose one by the odd goal. The club's first scorer on artificial surface was David Buchanan in the 1-1 draw with the Latics on 11 October 1986. Sunderland also played one game on Preston North End's artificial surface at Deepdale where goals from Gates and McPhail gave them a 2-2 draw.

PLAY-OFFS
Sunderland have been involved in the play-offs at the end of the season on three occasions.

In 1986-87 Sunderland finished the season in 19th place in the Second Division and so entered into a two leg play-off with Third Division Gillingham to decide which club would proceed to a final play-off to decide promotion and relegation issues.

In the first leg at at Priestfield Stadium, the Wearsiders lost 3-2 due to a second half hat-trick from Tony Cascarino and some dreadful errors by the usually reliable goalkeeper Iain Hesford. In the return at Roker Park, the visitors added to their overall lead with a third minute goal, but two goals from Eric Gates brought the scores level. In the 33rd minute Sunderland were awarded a penalty but the Gillingham 'keeper made a fine save. Hesford in the Sunderland goal then conceded a penalty, but then made amends by saving the spot-kick. Unfortunately, Cascarino followed up to put Gillingham ahead 5-4 on aggregate. With just two minutes to go, Gary Bennett equalised to take the tie into extra-time.

Republic of Ireland international Cascarino made it 3-3 on the night and 6-5 on aggregate, and though Bertschin scored for Sunderland, the Wearsiders lost on the away goals rule despite winning their home leg 4-3. Sunderland were relegated to the Third Division for the first time in their history.

After finishing sixth in Division Two in 1989-90, Sunderland were paired with neighbours and rivals Newcastle United in a two leg semi-final play-off. The first leg at Roker Park ended goalless although Sunderland's Paul Hardyman missed a penalty. At St James' Park, goals from Eric Gates and Marco Gabbiadini silenced the home fans and took Sunderland through to the Wembley play-off final against Swindon Town. The Wiltshire club totally dominated the game and won 1-0, though it would have been a much wider margin if Tony Norman hadn't been in such good form. However, the County Ground club were found guilty by both the Inland Revenue and Football Association for dealings which took place under the previous management and were relegated, with Sunderland taking their place in the First Division.

The club were last involved in the play-off finals in 1997-98 after finishing third in Division One. Despite losing 2-1 at Sheffield United in the first leg of the semi-final play-off, a 2-0 win in front of 40,092 at the Stadium of Light took the Wearsiders through to the final at Wembley, where their opponents were Charlton Athletic. Both games in the league had ended all square so the 77,739 crowd knew it was going to be a closely contested game. In a see-saw match, Clive Mendonca gave the Londoners the lead after 23 minutes, his strike proving to be the only goal of the first half. Niall Quinn equalised five minutes after the restart before Kevin Phillips shot Sunderland into the lead in the 58th minute. Mendonca scored his and Charlton's second in the 71st minute but two minutes later, Quinn had restored the Wearsiders' lead. With just five minutes to go, Rufus scored Charlton's third and equalising goal to take the tie into extra time. Nicky Summerbee put Sunderland ahead but Clive Mendonca then drew his side level and in doing so, became the first player to score a hat-trick in a play-off final. The game went to penalties which Charlton won 7-6 to take their place in the Premiership.

POINTS

Under the three points for a win system which was introduced in 1981-82, Sunderland's best points tally is 105 points in 1998-99 when the club won the First Division Championship. However, the club's best points haul under the old two points for a win system was 61 in 1963-64 when the Wearsiders finished runners-up in the Second Division.

Sunderland's worst record under either system was the meagre 23 points secured in season's 1890-91 and 1896-97. However, they were from 22 and 30 match programmes respectively.

The club's lowest from a 42 match programme is 26 points in 1969-70 when they finished 21st in the First Division and were relegated.

PORTERFIELD, IAN

Ian Porterfield's place in the folklore of Sunderland Football Club is assured by virtue of the goal he scored to give the then Second Division club a memorable FA Cup Final victory over Leeds United in 1973.

A product of Dunfermline, he began his career with Raith Rovers before joining Sunderland in December 1967 for a fee of £45,000. He made his debut for the Wearsiders in the last game of that year in a 3-3 draw at home to arch rivals Newcastle United. An intelligent midfield player, he was a Sunderland regular for the next seven seasons and went on to play in 270 games for the club. Misfortune followed his glory, for in December 1974 he suffered a fractured jaw in a car crash and it was only his determination that saved his career.

After a loan spell at Reading he joined Sheffield Wednesday and gave the Owls excellent service over almost three years before leaving in January 1980 to begin a career in management.

He led Rotherham United to the Third Division championship before leaving to join Fourth Division Sheffield United. The Blades won the title at the end of his first season in charge and in 1983-84 they were promoted again to the Second Division. Despite a good record at Bramall Lane, he was sacked and replaced Alex Ferguson as manager of Aberdeen. They reached the semi-finals of the Scottish Cup and the League Cup Final in 1987-88 where they lost to Rangers on penalties. He had little success as manager of Reading before replacing Bobby Campbell as manager of

Chelsea. He lost his job at Stamford Bridge in February 1993 after a poor run in which the London club went without a win in 12 games. He then joined Bolton Wanderers as first team coach but later lost the job.

Ian Porterfield

PREMIER LEAGUE

After winning the First Division Championship in 1995-96, Sunderland's manager Peter Reid was determined that the club's stay in the Premiership was not a short one. During the close season he made ten signings, with Republic of Ireland international Niall Quinn the most expensive at £1.3 million, though injury ruled out most of his season.

In what was to be the club's final season at Roker Park, the Wearsiders started the campaign reasonably well, suffering only two defeats in the opening seven matches. However, after that inconsistency set in and the side never won two consecutive games. Despite that the club's home form was quite good and at the turn of the year they went five games undefeated including a 1-0 victory over Arsenal. In February 1997 the club lost four successive matches, the first three by a 1-0 scoreline before Spurs won 4-0 at Roker Park! The club drew 1-1 with rivals Newcastle United at St James' Park but then lost 2-1 to Liverpool to enter the bottom three for the first time. The club appeared to have a lifeline after a 1-0 victory at Middlesbrough but then a 1-0 defeat at home to Southampton piled on the pressure. The Wearsider's final home game at Roker Park saw them beat Everton 3-0 to complete their only double of the campaign. Sadly the victory could not prevent the club's relegation after just one season of Premier League football as an 85th minute goal at Wimbledon on the last day of the season coupled with Coventry City's win at White Hart Lane sent Sunderland down.

PROCTOR, MARK

Middlesbrough-born Mark Proctor had a trial with Leeds United when he was 14 but returned to Teeside homesick after only three days at Elland Road and signed associate schoolboy forms for Middlesbrough.

Proctor captained the England Youth side in an international tournament in Los Palmas before becoming a full-time professional with Middlesbrough in September 1978. After making two appearances for England at Under-21 level and scoring 14 goals in 125 games, he left Ayresome Park in August 1981 and signed for Nottingham Forest for £440,000. He won two more Under-21 caps whilst at the City Ground but following a loan spell with Sunderland, he signed for the Wearsiders on a permanent basis, for a fee of £80,000 in the summer of 1983. He went on to score 23 goals in 139 League and Cup games for the north-east club before Sheffield Wednesday paid £275,000 for his services in September 1987. After just 59 league appearances for the Owls, Proctor made a surprise return to Middlesbrough midway through the 1988-89 season but arrived too late to save the club from relegation.

PROMOTION

Sunderland have been promoted on seven occasions. The Wearsiders were first promoted in 1963-64 when they finished runners-up to Leeds United in the Second Division. Losing just six games, the club had to wait until the final home game of the season when Johnny Crossan netted his 22nd goal in a 2-1 win over Charlton Athletic before knowing their fate.

Sunderland's next promotion came in 1975-76 and was again from the

Second to the First Division but this time as champions. They were undefeated at home, winning 19 and drawing two of their fixtures.

Sunderland were next promoted in 1979-80 with the club again going through the season undefeated at home. The club's fourth promotion was in 1987-88 as the Wearsiders won the Third Division championship after just one season in that section, securing a record 93 points. The Wearsiders were promoted for a fifth time in 1989-90 but in rather unusual circumstances. Having finished sixth in the Second Division, they reached the final of the play-offs but lost 1-0 to Swindon Town. They were resigned to facing another season of Second Division football when Swindon were found guilty of financial irregularities and relegated, with Sunderland taking their place. The club were promoted for a sixth time in 1998-99 when they won the First Division Championship. They began the season with an unbeaten run of 18 matches and ended the campaign with 105 points, losing just three of their 46 matches.

PURDON, TED

After coming to England with the Maritz Brothers soccer team of Johannesburg, Ted Purdon was one of seven South Africans taken on at Birmingham City but the only one to make a name for himself.

Purdon played his early football in Pretoria and joined the Maritz team in 1948, scoring over 50 goals in his first two seasons. He scored on his debut for the St Andrews club against Leeds United and scored twice on his last appearance for the Blues against Rotherham United. He had scored 30 goals in 70 games for Birmingham when he left for Sunderland in January 1954.

He scored twice on his debut for the Wearsiders in a 5-0 home win over Cardiff City and then in his next match netted his only ever hat-trick in the top flight as Sunderland beat Arsenal 4-1 at Highbury. He went on to score 42 goals in 96 League and Cup games for the north-east club before joining Workington. He later served Barrow, Bath City, Bristol Rovers and Toronto City before returning to his native South Africa where he is now a successful businessman.

Q

QUINN, NIALL

Before starting his footballing career, Niall Quinn excelled at both Gaelic football and hurling. He was playing junior football in his native Ireland for Manortown United when Arsenal signed him in November 1983. In his first two seasons at Highbury he was a consistent member of Arsenal's youth side and went on to gain Republic of Ireland youth honours. After progressing through the reserve ranks, he scored on his Arsenal league debut against Liverpool in December 1985.

In 1986-87 his persistence gained him a regular place in the Arsenal league side and it was his equalising goal in the League Cup semi-final second leg against Tottenham Hotspur which helped Arsenal to the final that year. Following the arrival of Alan Smith, Quinn became a fringe member of the first team squad and in March 1990 Arsenal accepted an offer of £800,000 for his services from Manchester City.

Very few forwards cause more havoc in the air than Quinn and this coupled with his fantastic workrate, neat distribution and the superb way he holds up the ball, have made him into one of the best forwards in Europe.

At Maine Road, Quinn averaged a goal every third game but during the 1996 close season he left to join Sunderland for £1.3 million, the club's record signing. The Republic of Ireland international who has won 63 caps and represented his country in two World Cups made his debut for the Wearsiders as a substitute in a goalless draw at home to Leicester City on the opening day of the 1996-97 season. He started the campaign well, finding the net three times in his first seven starts before an ankle injury ruled him out of first team action for seven months. It looked as though the popular Irishman was going to miss the bulk of the 1997-98 season as well following a third knee operation in a year in September 1997 but he thankfully returned to first team action in November and formed a prolific partnership with Kevin Phillips. Having scored the first goal at the Stadium of Light in a 3-1 win over his former club, Manchester City, he went on to score 14 league goals including a hat-trick in a 4-1 home win over Stockport County. He also scored twice in the play-off final at Wembley which Sunderland lost 7-6 on penalties after drawing 4-4 with Charlton Athletic. In 1998-99, Quinn had a magnificent season, scoring some memorable goals in the club's First Division Championship-winning season.

Niall Quinn

R

RAPID SCORING
When Sunderland beat top of the table Newcastle United 9-1 at St James' Park on 5 December 1908, they scored eight goals in 28 minutes including the last five in eight minutes! The club's scorers that day were Billy Hogg (3) George Holley (3) Arthur Bridgett (2) and Jackie Mordue.

RECEIPTS
The club's record receipts are £605,310 for the visit of Sheffield United in a First Division play-off match on 13 May 1998. For the record, a crowd of 40,092 saw Sunderland win 2-0 to take the tie 3-2 on aggregate.

REFEREES
When Sunderland entertained Derby County at Roker Park on the opening day of the 1894-95 First Division campaign, the referee failed to arrive and the match started with a linesman officiating. At half-time, Sunderland were winning 3-0 but then the referee arrived and the teams agreed to start again. Sunderland proceeded to win 8-0 officially (11-0 unofficially!).

REID, PETER
Peter Reid was a member of the successful Huyton Boys side that caused something of a stir when they won the English Schools Trophy in 1970. A number of clubs offered him the chance to become an apprentice but Reid opted for Bolton Wanderers and in October 1974 he made his first team debut

as a substitute in a home match against Orient. An ever-present for the next two seasons, his cultured midfield play and his intense desire to be involved at all times, were features of Bolton's Second Division championship-winning side of 1977-78. That season also saw him appear in England's Under-21 side but just as his career seemed to be taking off, he suffered the misfortune of a broken leg. On New Year's Day 1979, he collided with Everton goalkeeper George Wood in a game which was later abandoned.

Contractual problems prevented the midfielder from playing after he failed to agree terms with Arsenal, Everton and Wolverhampton Wanderers. Eventually he was placed on a weekly contract but in September 1981 he broke his leg again in a match against Barnsley. Again he regained full fitness and in December 1982 became one of the bargain buys of all-time when he joined Everton for £60,000.

Peter Reid

In 1984-85 came Everton's finest hour. They came very close to the treble of League, FA Cup and European Cup Winners' Cup and Reid was voted the Footballers' Player of the Year. When he replaced the injured Bryan Robson in the World Cup Finals of 1986, the previously ineffective England side took on a new life and there is no doubt that had he spent less time in plaster, he would have been a major force at international level. On the departure of Howard Kendall in the summer of 1987, Reid became player-coach, a role he fulfilled until he joined Queen's Park Rangers later that year.

Following Kendall's appointment as manager of Manchester City, Reid moved to Maine Road as player-coach and in November 1990 following Kendall's return to Goodison Park, he became manager. After leaving Maine Road he was appointed manager of Sunderland in March 1995, the club's fifth change in a little over three years.

In his first full season at Roker Park he led the club to the First Division Championship and was voted Manager of the Year. Though he was determined to see that Sunderland did not repeat their previous visit to the top flight which expired after just one season, the club's last season at Roker Park did end in relegation. In 1997-98 Sunderland finished third in Division One but lost out to Charlton Athletic in a penalty shoot-out in the play-off final at Wembley. In 1998-99, Reid's Sunderland won the First Division Championship with a massive 105 points.

Sunderland's full league record under Peter Reid is:

P	W	D	L	F	A
183	92	54	37	278	169

RELEGATION

Sunderland have been relegated on seven occasions. Their first taste came in 1957-58 in what was Alan Brown's first season as manager. The club who were relegated along with Sheffield Wednesday had been in the First Division since 1890 and were the last Football League club able to claim the distinction of playing solely in the First Division.

They were next relegated in 1969-70 after just six seasons back in the top flight and again went down with Sheffield Wednesday.

The club were relegated for a third time in 1976-77. Having regained their First Division status in 1980-81, the Wearsiders spent just one season in Division One before returning to the Second Division. They went through one spell during the season of nine consecutive defeats and though they rallied, losing only twice in 16 games, Sunderland needed to draw at Everton in the final game to stay up. They lost 2-0 and entered the Second Division for a third spell.

In 1984-85 Sunderland were relegated for a fourth time after returning to the First Division in 1979-80 but worse was to follow two seasons later when the club were relegated to the Third Division for the first time in their history. After finishing 19th in the Second Division, Sunderland were involved in the play-offs and faced Gillingham in a two-leg match. After losing 3-2 at the Priestfield Stadium, Sunderland won 4-3 at home but went out on the away goals rule.

The club were next relegated in 1990-91 when, despite a reasonable start, they ended the campaign in 19th place.

The club's seventh and final experience came in 1996-97 when the Wearsiders lost their Premier League status after just one season in the top flight.

In what was the club's last season at Roker Park, a 1-0 defeat at Wimbledon on the final day of the season, coupled with Coventry City's win at Tottenham Hotspur sent Sunderland down.

REVIE, DON

Don Revie began his Football League career with Leicester City but took some time to be appreciated by the Filbert Street crowd. However, his performances in the club's run to the 1949 FA Cup Final, where he scored two goals in the semi-final victory over Portsmouth won them over. Sadly he missed the Wembley game due to broken blood vessels in his nose.

He was sold to Hull City in November 1949 for £20,000 but lost his form and was switched to wing-half to recover some confidence. After player-manager Raich Carter left Boothferry Park, Revie requested a transfer and in October 1951 joined Manchester City for £25,000. At Maine Road he was the tactical architect of what became known as the 'Revie Plan'. Revie played as a deep-lying centre-forward who prompted his inside-forwards rather than playing in the traditional style of an out-and-out striker. He masterminded City's 1956 FA Cup Final triumph against Birmingham and won six England caps before a fee of £22,000 took him to Sunderland in 1956.

He made his debut in a 1-0 defeat at Cardiff City on 17 November 1956 and though injuries hampered his first season at Roker Park, he returned to full fitness for the 1957-58 season, scoring 12 goals in 39 games. Sadly, Sunderland were relegated to the Second Division for the first time in their history and in November 1958 he joined Leeds United for £12,000.

He enjoyed a brief spell as captain before being appointed player-manager in March 1961, retiring as a player in the 1963 close season. Revie, who was Footballer of the Year in 1955, developed a youth policy at Elland Road and in 1963-64 the Yorkshire club powered their way to the Second Division title. United made an immediate impact in the First Division and in ten years in the top flight they won two League titles, the FA Cup, the Football League Cup and the Fairs Cup twice, plus a string of near misses. During his reign at Elland Road, Revie was named Manager of the Year in 1969, 1970 and 1972 and was awarded the OBE in January 1970.

In July 1974 he left Elland Road to become England's manager but unable to recapture the club atmosphere at international level, he left to become coach to the United Arab Emirates on a tax-free contract reputed to be £60,000 per year. His move was bitterly criticised by the FA

Don Revie

who suspended him from working in England until he was willing to face a charge of bringing the game into disrepute. He later won a High Court case against the FA and was granted an injunction quashing the ban, though many considered it a hollow victory. He later took up a consulting post at Elland Road but in the late 1980s he was struck down by a motor neurone disease and in later years was confined to a wheelchair, dying in Murrayfield Hospital, Edinburgh on 26 May 1989.

REYNOLDS, TOM

Speedy winger Tom Reynolds joined the Wearsiders from Felling Juniors in the summer of 1946. Though he made nearly all his appearances for the club at outside-left, he made his debut on the right-wing in a disastrous 5-0 defeat at Charlton Athletic on 11 September 1946. He won a regular place in the club's first team at the start of the 1947-48 season and over the next five seasons was an important member of the Sunderland side. In 1949-50 when the club finished third in Division One, Reynolds was ever-present, scoring five goals. However, he created many more for the likes of Dickie Davis and Ivor Broadis with his measured passes and pin-point crosses.

Reynolds who scored 18 goals in 171 League and Cup games for Sunderland, played his last game for the club in a 5-1 defeat at Burnley in April 1953. After a season and a half playing reserve team football, he joined Darlington in December 1954 and went on to score six goals in 42 league games for the Quakers.

ROBINSON, JACKIE

Sheffield Wednesday manager Billy Walker discovered Jackie Robinson playing in a junior match on Tyneside in 1934 and was so impressed that he brought him to Hillsborough immediately. Within weeks of gaining a regular place in the Wednesday side in 1936, he was playing in an international trial match and a year later, scored on his full international debut in an 8-0 win over Finland in Helsinki. That was the first of four caps that Robinson won.

He was just reaching his peak in 1938-39 when the Second World War interrupted his progress. Yet it is for his feats in the war years that the Shiremoor-born player is best remembered. In just over 100 games, he scored 90 goals with his tally being 35 in 1942-43, a total which included six hat-tricks. There were some of his team-mates who insisted that he gave his better performances after he had had a few pints before the game!

Surprisingly in October 1946 he was sold to Sunderland for £7,500. The fee was subsequently reduced when it was revealed Robinson was two years older than everybody had thought.

He scored on his debut for the Wearsiders in a 2-1 home defeat by Grimsby Town and ended the campaign with 18 goals in 31 games including four in a 5-0 win at Blackpool. He went on to score 34 goals in 85 League and Cup appearances before moving to Lincoln City in the summer of 1949. However, a broken leg after only eight games for the Sincil Bank club ended his playing days.

ROBSON, BRYAN

Better known as 'Pop', Bryan Robson began his football career with Newcastle United where he won a Second Division Championship medal, an Inter Cities Fairs Cup winners' medal and two England Under-23 caps. He had scored 82 goals in 206 league games for the Magpies when he signed for West Ham United for a club record fee of £120,000 in February 1971. In 1972-73 he scored 28 league goals, including a hat-trick in a 4-3 win over Southampton to make him the league's equal top scorer with Exeter City's

Bryan Robson

Fred Binney. At the end of the 1973-74 season he returned to his native north-east to join Sunderland.

An ever-present in his first season with the Wearsiders, scoring 19 goals in 42 games, he helped the club win promotion to the First Division in 1974-75 as Second Division champions but in October 1976 he returned to Upton Park to join the Hammers. In 1978-79 he topped the Second Division scoring charts with 24 goals, netting a hat-trick in a 3-0 home win over Millwall and winning the Adidas Golden Boot award. Although he was offered a new contract, he returned to play for Sunderland for the second time in the summer of 1979. Top-scoring with 20 goals, he won another Second Division Championship medal in 1979-80 but then joined Carlisle United and had a spell at Chelsea before returning to Roker Park for a third time as the club's player-coach. He took his total of goals scored to 67 in 181 first team games before being appointed manager of Carlisle United. He later relinquished the post to play for Gateshead in the Northern Premier League before later coaching at Manchester United. He is now back with the Wearsiders as Youth Team Coach.

ROKER PARK

Roker Park was opened on 10 September 1898 in front of Sunderland's highest ever home gate of around 30,000. The visitors were Liverpool, with Tom Watson, Sunderland's first manager's new club!

Before the match got underway, the club's President, the Marquis of Londonderry opened a small gate leading from the dressing rooms onto the playing surface with a golden key. For the record, Sunderland won 1-0 with Jim Leslie scoring the all-important goal.

On 18 February 1899 the ground staged its first international when England played Ireland. Sadly a crowd of only 10,000 saw England win 13-2, still the country's record score in internationals.

Roker Park had originally been farmland owned by a Mr Tennant and he only allowed Sunderland to become his tenants on condition that their presence wouldn't interfere with his plans to have houses built on the rest of the site. In 1908 the club decided to purchase the freehold for £10,000 and four years later the club made its first ground improvement when the Roker End, a wooden terrace was replaced by a structure that, for a cost of £6,000 allowed the players to train 'under' the Roker End should the weather be inclement. The alteration also meant that the ground's capacity was now 50,000, which when the Fulwell End was expanded in 1925 raised it even further to 60,000.

In 1929, Scottish engineer Archibald Leitch, who had designed the new stand with concrete supports at the Roker End, built a new Main Stand. It featured his familiar criss-cross steelwork balcony and housed 5,875 seats on its upper tier. The stand which cost £25,000 was opened on 7 September 1929 for the visit of Manchester City, a game which Sunderland won 5-2 with Dave Halliday scoring a hat-trick.

On 8 March 1933 the ground housed its largest ever crowd when 75,118 crammed into Roker Park for the FA Cup fourth round replay against Derby County.

After the club won the League Championship in 1935-36, they decided to replace the original Clock Stand, the new one, which was opened by Lady Raine on 2 September 1936, holding 15,500 standing spectators.

During the Second World War, bombs fell onto the playing surface and behind the Roker End, killing a policeman and damaging a small club house.

In 1950, the upper section of the Main Stand was converted into seating. Two years later, Roker Park became only the second top flight ground (Highbury being the first) to have floodlights, and on 11 December 1952 they were switched on for a friendly game against Dundee.

Roker Park
Home of Sunderland FC until 1997

In 1966, Roker Park was chosen to stage three Group Four games in the World Cup and also the quarter-final match between Hungary and USSR. This necessitated the pitch being lengthened by three yards, seats installed at the rear of the Clock Stand and temporary seats added to the Fulwell End and the paddocks. The costs for there alterations were met by a loan from the FA and government grants.

After the club had won the FA Cup in 1973, executive boxes were added to the Main Stand at Roker Park which now had a capacity of 58,000. However, in 1977, £250,000 had to be spent on improvements following Roker being designated under the Safety of Sports Grounds Act, and the capacity was cut to 47,077.

Five years later the ground capacity was cut by a further 10,000 after part of the Roker End had to be demolished. In 1989 in wake of the Hillsborough disaster, this figure was reduced to 31,639, but when the Taylor Report was published in 1990 the club decided to review the situation regarding ground improvements.

After further reductions in the capacity, Sunderland chairman Bob Murray and the board looked into possible sites for relocating the club and once they had decided on a move to the Stadium of Light, the Wearsiders played their last match at Roker Park against Everton on 3 May 1997, which they won 3-0.

ROOSE, LEIGH

Doctor Leigh Richmond Roose was one of the most famous amateur players of the pre-First World War period and was for many years Wales' most capped goalkeeper, playing 24 times for them between 1900 and 1911. As an amateur he played for a variety of clubs and signed for different sides at different times for different leagues.

Roose was a wealthy man and on one occasion he hired his own train to get him to an Aston Villa match. He started at Ruabon Druids and played for Aberystwyth and London Welsh before joining Stoke in October 1901.

He then spent three seasons at Stoke, before moving on to Everton. However, his stay at Goodison was short and he rejoined Stoke. In January 1908 he moved to Sunderland and played his first game for the club in a 3-2 defeat at Preston North End.

After that he was a virtual ever-present and in 1908-09 when the club finished third in Division One, he missed just three games. In those three games, his deputy Robert Allan conceded 14 goals including eight at

Blackburn Rovers. He went on to play in 99 games and made his final Welsh international appearance in March 1911 against Scotland at Cardiff.

He went on to play for Huddersfield Town, Aston Villa, Woolwich Arsenal, Aberystwyth Town and Llandudno Town before retiring in 1915. He joined the Royal Fusiliers and won the Military Medal before he was killed in action in France on 7 October 1916, aged 38.

ROSTRON, WILF

When his studying allowed, Wilf Rostron played for Arsenal's South East Counties League side as an amateur during 1972-73. After a number of impressive performances in Arsenal's Combination League side, he made his league debut against Newcastle United at Highbury in March 1975. Over the next three seasons he appeared in just 19 League and Cup games, being unable to command a regular place in the Gunners' side.

In August 1977 he joined Sunderland for a fee of £30,000 and made his debut four months later in a 3-0 home win over Burnley. Over the next two seasons, Rostron played in a variety of positions for the club and in April 1979 scored a spectacular hat-trick in a 6-2 home win over

Wilf Rostron

Sheffield United. He had scored 18 goals in 93 games for the Wearsiders before joining Watford in October 1979.

At Vicarage Road, Rostron was instrumental in helping the Hornets win promotion to the First Division and reach the 1984 FA Cup Final. He had played in 317 league games for Watford when he moved to Sheffield Wednesday in January 1989 and later Sheffield United in the same year. He then joined Brentford as a player and later became coach.

ROWELL, GARY

The son of a professional footballer, Gary Rowell joined Sunderland as an apprentice and signed as a professional soon after he turned 17 in 1974. He made his league debut in a 1-0 home win over Oxford United in December 1975 but was unable to claim a regular first team place in a Wearsiders' team on its way to the Second Division championship in 1976.

Despite Sunderland being relegated in 1976-77, his first full season, Rowell impressed enough to win an England Under-21 cap against Finland in Helsinki in May 1977.

Gary Rowell arrived as a prolific marksman in 1977 and he was top

Gary Rowell

scorer at Roker Park in four of his next six seasons, hitting hat-tricks against Newcastle United (Away 4-1) in 1978-79 and Arsenal (Home 3-0) in 1982-83. After scoring 101 goals in 305 games he was transferred to Norwich City in 1984 but hardly played at all in an injury-plagued season at Carrow Road. He returned to his native north-east with Middlesbrough in the summer of 1985 but after just one season in which he was the club's top scorer with ten goals, he was released with 'Boro destined for Third Division football.

He then had spells with Brighton, Dundee and Carlisle United before ending his league career with Burnley.

RUNNERS-UP

Sunderland have been First Division runners-up on five occasions. The table below shows the club's points record in relation to the season's champions:

1893-94	Aston Villa 44	Sunderland 38
1897-98	Sheffield United 42	Sunderland 37
1900-01	Liverpool 45	Sunderland 43
1922-23	Liverpool 60	Sunderland 54
1934-35	Arsenal 58	Sunderland 54

RUSSELL, CRAIG

A life-long Sunderland fan, South Shields-born Craig Russell made his debut for the Wearsiders in a 2-1 home defeat by Southend United on 30 November 1991. However, it wasn't until 1993-94 that he established himself as a first team regular. Though he scored a number of important goals prior to 1995-96, it was that First Division championship-winning season when he found the net on a regular basis and ended the campaign as the club's leading scorer with 13 goals in 35 games. The highlight of that season was his four goals in the 6-0 home demolition of Millwall.

Surprisingly he spent most of the club's 1996-97 Premier League season on the substitutes' bench, a strange situation, especially as the club struggled to score goals. Despite only making ten starts in the Premiership, he ended the season as joint-top scorer with four goals!

Following the arrival of Kevin Phillips from Watford, Russell found himself out of favour and in November 1997 after scoring 34 goals in 174 games, he joined Manchester City with Nicky Summerbee going in the opposite direction in a straight swop.

S

SECOND DIVISION

Sunderland have had six spells in the Second Division. Their first began in 1958-59 following their relegation from the First Division the previous campaign after 57 seasons of playing top flight football. It lasted for six seasons until 1963-64 when they returned to the First Division as runners-up to Leeds United. The Wearsiders lost their First Division status again in 1969-70 and had another spell of six seasons in the Second Division before winning the championship with 56 points in 1975-76.

They only spent one season in the First Division before returning for a third spell of Second Division football in 1977-78. However, after just three seasons, the club won promotion as runners-up to Leicester City, having gone through the campaign undefeated at home. After five seasons of mid-table placings in Division One, the club were relegated in 1984-85 and began their fourth spell of Second Division football the following season. After two seasons of near relegation to the Third Division the Wearsiders were eventually relegated in 1986-87 when they lost over two legs to Gillingham in the play-offs at the end of the season.

The club won promotion at the first attempt, ending the season as Third Division Champions and so in 1988-89 began their fifth spell in the Second Division. In 1989-90 they finished sixth in the Second Division and were involved in the end of season play-offs. After beating Newcastle United over two legs, the club met Swindon Town at Wembley and though they lost 1-0 on the day, they gained a First Division place at the expense of the Wiltshire club who were relegated following an investigation into financial irregularities at the County Ground.

After just one season, the north-east club found themselves back in Division Two and had spent two seasons at that level when the Football League underwent reorganisation and they began the 1992-93 campaign in the new First Division.

Sunderland's Second Division Championship-winning side of 1975-76

SHACKLETON, LEN
After Arsenal had rejected him as a youngster, Len Shackleton joined his local club, Bradford Park Avenue as the Second World War began.

In October 1946 he left the Yorkshire club to join Newcastle United who paid £13,000 for him. He made a most spectacular debut for the Magpies, scoring six goals in United's 13-0 thrashing of Newport County including three in the space of two-and-a-half minutes, which is believed to be the fastest first-class hat-trick of all-time. He went on to score 29 goals in 64 games for the Magpies including taking part in the first half of the club's 1947-48 promotion campaign, before a shake-up within the club saw him join Sunderland in February 1948 for a fee of £20,050.

He made his debut for the Wearsiders in a 5-1 defeat at Derby County on 14 February 1948 and over the next ten seasons scored 101 goals in 348 games including a hat-trick in a 3-0 home win over Manchester City in August 1951.

One of the game's most entertaining players, Shackleton was a skilful inside-forward who had few peers, although there were occasions when he set out to please the paying public, sometimes at the expense of his own team! Shackleton, who was nicknamed 'The Clown Prince of Soccer' won six caps for England, the first against Wales in 1949. There were many who thought that he should be an England regular but his international appearances were restricted because of his unwillingness to conform!

He was a great favourite with the Sunderland fans and they were sad-dened when an ankle injury forced his retirement in September 1957.

A great humourist, a chapter in his autobiography was entitled 'What the average director knows about football' - Shackleton left the page blank!

SHARKEY, NICK

A Scottish Schoolboy international, Nick Sharkey made his Sunderland debut in a 1-0 home win over Scunthorpe United on 9 April 1960. It was his only appearance that season and though he went on to score 15 goals in 24 League and Cup games over the next three seasons, it was 1963-64 before he won a regular place in the Wearsiders' first team.

On 20 March 1963, Sharkey hit the headlines when he scored five of Sunderland's goals in a 7-1 win over Norwich City. In 1963-64 he scored 17 goals in 33 games including a hat-trick in a 6-0 defeat of Swindon Town to help the Wearsiders win promotion to the First Division as runners-up to Leeds United. The following season, Sharkey continued to score on a regular basis netting 18 goals in 32 games as the club finished 15th on their return to the top flight. He had scored 62 goals in 120 games for the Wearside club when he left to join Leicester City for £15,000 in October 1966.

He never really settled at Leicester and signed for Mansfield Town after just six league appearances and five goals in 18 months with the Filberts. After scoring 17 goals in 69 league games for the Stags, he returned to the north-east to end his league career with Hartlepool United where he scored 12 goals in 60 games.

SHAW, HAROLD

Left-back Harold Shaw played his early football with his home-town team of Hednesford, making the first team at the age of 15. Wolves' manager George Jobey signed him in the summer of 1923 and he went straight into the first team, winning a Third Division (North) Championship medal in 1923-24. He missed only five league games in that campaign and was a first team regular with the Molineux club for the next decade. He had played in 249 first team games for Wolves when Major Frank Buckley surprised all their supporters by selling Shaw to Sunderland for just over £7,000 in February 1930.

He made his debut for the Wearsiders in the local derby against Newcastle United at St James' Park in a match Sunderland lost 3-0. He was ever-present in 1931-32 and scored the first goal of his career in a 4-2 defeat at Everton after having failed to find the net during his career with Wolves. In fact, he netted another in the 4-1 home win over Leicester City that season and ended his Sunderland career with five goals in 217 League and Cup games.

He was with Sunderland when they won the League Championship in 1935-36 but played only once that season in what turned out to be the last league game of his career. He was on the sidelines when the Wearsiders won the FA Cup the following season.

SIDDALL, BARRY

Having appeared in Bolton Wanderers' Central League side whilst still at school, the Ellesmere Port-born goalkeeper went on to win England Youth honours before making his league debut for the Lancashire club at Walsall in October 1972. Following the retirement of Charlie Wright, Siddall made a great impact on the club's return to the Second Division and went on to appear in 133 consecutive league games. After appearing in 158 games for the Wanderers, Siddall joined Sunderland in September 1976 for £80,000.

He made his debut in a 1-0 home defeat by Aston Villa and went on to appear in 103 consecutive league games immediately following his first appearance. He played in 189 League and Cup games for the then Roker Park club and after a loan spell at Darlington, he joined Port Vale. Loan spells at Blackpool and Stoke City followed before a permanent transfer to the Potters for £20,000. He went on loan to Tranmere Rovers and Manchester City before signing for Blackpool in the summer of 1986 on a free transfer. He later played for Stockport County, Hartlepool United, Carlisle United, Chester City and Preston North End, eventually taking his total of league appearances for this much travelled 'keeper to 613.

Barry Siddall

SIMOD CUP
The Simod Cup replaced the Full Members' Cup in the 1987-88 season, though it was 1988-89 before Sunderland participated in the competition. A goal from Marco Gabbiadini gave the Wearsiders a 1-0 win at Charlton Athletic in the first round and though the Nottingham-born striker was on the scoresheet again in the next round, the club went down 2-1 at Blackburn Rovers.

SMALLEST PLAYER
Although such statistics are always unreliable for those playing before the turn of the century, it appears that the distinction of being Sunderland's smallest player goes to Ernie Taylor. Though he stood at 5ft 4ins, no player displayed more courage or tenacity or the ability to split defences wide open with one devastating pass.

SMITH, DENIS
Idolised by the Stoke public for his total commitment, he overcame countless injuries and broken bones to establish himself in the number five shirt, which he was to make his own.

161

After making his City debut against Arsenal at Highbury in September 1968 he won a regular place alongside Alan Bloor in the heart of the Stoke defence. Not the most cultured of defenders, there were nonetheless not too many strikers who enjoyed playing against him. On 23 February 1974 he scored the winning goal against Leeds United as Stoke came from two goals down to win 3-2 and end the Elland Road side's record-breaking run of games without defeat. Though he represented the Football League, a full international cap eluded him. However, he won a winners' medal in 1972 as the Potters won the League Cup. Towards the end of his playing career he joined the Stoke coaching staff and earned a well-deserved testimonial from the club.

After leaving Stoke where he made 407 league appearances, he embarked on a career in management with York City. Along with his right-hand man Viv Busby, they took York to their first major trophy in the club's history when they won the Fourth Division championship in 1983-84.

Sunderland paid York £20,000 when Smith and Busby moved to Roker Park in the summer of 1987. They clinched the Third Division title in their first season at the club, then made the Second Division play-offs in 1990. They lost to Swindon in the final but were promoted when the Wiltshire club were relegated after an illegal betting scandal. The club lasted just one season in the top flight and when they struggled in the Second Division, Smith was sacked.

After ten months in charge of Bristol City, he was dismissed as the Ashton Gate club struggled at the wrong end of the table. He then took charge at Oxford United but in December 1997 after four years at the Manor Ground, he became manager of West Bromwich Albion.

Sunderland's full league record under Denis Smith is:

P	W	D	L	F	A
204	80	57	67	295	270

SPONSORS
The club's current sponsors are Lambton's whilst previous sponsors have included Vaux Breweries and Cowies.

STADIUM OF LIGHT
Situated at Monkwearmouth, the former colliery site is much closer to the town centre than Roker Park, and can be seen from both sides of the River Wear.

The stadium cost £14.5 million of which £3.25 million came from the Football Trust, plus £3.5 million worth of site preparation and infrastructure costs which was paid by the Development Corporation.

The ground has a single tier on three sides and a two-tier main stand and was first used for a Football League match on 15 August 1997 when a crowd of 38,894 saw the Wearsiders beat Manchester City 3-1.

The record attendance at the ground was set on 20 March 1999 when 41,505 witnessed a 3-1 win over Bolton Wanderers.

STELLING, JACK

Washington-born full-back Jack Stelling played his early football with Unsworth Colliery before signing for Sunderland in September 1944. Able to play on either flank, he appeared in 65 wartime games before making his Football League debut in a 3-2 home win over Derby County on the opening day of the 1946-47 season.

Over the next eight seasons, Stelling missed very few games and in 1949-50 when the Wearsiders finished the season in third place in Division One, Stelling was ever-present. During that season, Stelling scored five of the eight goals scored whilst wearing the colours of Sunderland, one of them a spectacular strike to win the game against Burnley.

A loyal one-club man, Jack Stelling went on to appear in 272 League and Cup games for the Wearsiders before retiring in May 1958 after playing his last first team game against Sheffield United in April 1956.

STOKOE, BOB

Bob Stokoe played his first game for Newcastle United on Christmas Day 1950 at centre-forward against Middlesbrough and scored a goal! After switching to centre-half he became a regular in the Magpies' side and went on to appear in 287 games for the club, gaining an FA Cup winners' medal in 1955 as United beat Manchester City 3-1. In December 1961 after 14 years on the St James' Park staff, Stokoe was appointed player-manager of Bury. He played in 81 league games for the Shakers before hanging up his boots.

Stokoe resigned from the Gigg Lane club in the summer of 1965 and took over at struggling Charlton Athletic. After selling two of the club's most popular players in Mike Bailey and Billy Bonds, Stokoe was sacked in September 1967, but he was paid compensation by the club after he had left.

The following month he was appointed manager of Rochdale but after helping the Lancashire club avoid re-election for the third season running,

Bob Stokoe

he resigned and took over at Carlisle United. After taking the Cumbrian side to the semi-finals of the League Cup, Stokoe left to become manager of Blackpool in December 1970 but was unable to prevent their relegation from the First Division. Though the Seasiders won the Anglo-Italian Trophy, he couldn't get the club back into the top flight and in November 1972 accepted an offer to manage Sunderland.

It was a great move for him, for at the end of his first season, the Roker Park club beat Leeds United 1-0 in the FA Cup Final at Wembley. Few will forget Stokoe charging across the pitch to hug Jim Montgomery at the final whistle, the keeper having made some memorable saves. Sunderland entered European competition for the first time but went out to Sporting Lisbon in the second round of the Cup Winners' Cup.

The Sunderland manager was busy in the transfer market bringing Dave Watson, Dennis Tueart and Tony Towers to Roker Park, and in 1975-76 he led the club back to the top flight as Second Division Champions. Sadly it all went wrong for him the following season and after just nine games in which the club had only taken four points, he resigned.

A year later he returned for his second spell as manager of Bury but it wasn't a happy time as the Lancashire club struggled in the lower reaches of the Third Division, and in May 1978 he resigned. He had another stint in charge of Blackpool but was sacked as the Bloomfield Road club failed to make much headway. He then had a second spell with Rochdale but they finished 92nd in the Football League and he left. Another of his former clubs, Carlisle United, appointed him manager, and in 1981-82 he took them back into the Second Division as runners-up to Burnley. He resigned his post at Brunton Park in May 1986. Stokoe returned to Roker Park as caretaker-manager from April to June 1987.

Sunderland's full league record under Bob Stokoe is:

P	W	D	L	F	A
168	78	41	49	247	165

SUBSTITUTES

The first-ever Sunderland substitute was Alan Gauden who came on for Mike Hellawell against Aston Villa at Villa Park on 6 September 1965. The club had to wait until 7 January 1967 for their first goalscoring substitute - George Herd scoring in the 1-1 draw against Blackpool at Bloomfield Road.

SUGGETT, COLIN

England Youth international Colin Suggett began his league career with Sunderland, making his debut in a 3-0 defeat at Stoke City in March 1967. He soon established himself with the Wearsiders and in 1967-68 was ever-present and the club's top scorer with 14 goals in the First Division. He missed very few games the following season but in June 1969 he left Roker Park after scoring 25 goals in 98 games to join West Bromwich Albion for £100,000.

He scored two goals on his debut for the Baggies at Southampton and in three and a half seasons at the Hawthorns scored 20 goals in 128 league outings before Norwich City manager John Bond paid a club record fee of £75,000 for his services.

He missed very few games in his five seasons at Carrow Road and in 1974-75 when the Canaries finished third in Division Two, he won the Barry Butler Memorial Trophy as the club's Player of the Year. He went on to score 28 goals in 236 League and Cup games before joining Newcastle United in the summer of 1978.

He had played in only 23 league games for the Magpies when an ankle ligament injury ended his career. He stayed at St James' Park for almost 16 years as youth team coach and caretaker manager before a row with the then United manager Kevin Keegan led to Suggett being sacked.

Colin Suggett

SUSTAINED SCORING

During the 1928-29 season when the club finished fourth in Division One, Dave Halliday scored 43 goals in 42 league games. He scored Sunderland's goal on the opening day of the season as they lost 3-1 at Burnley and two games later scored the first of four hat-tricks in a 4-0 home win over Derby County. Midway through the season he scored 11 goals in five consecutive games including a hat-trick against Manchester United (Home 5-1) and all four goals in a 4-4 draw at home to Sheffield United. His last hat-trick came in the penultimate game of the season as West Ham United were beaten 4-1 in front of a Roker Park crowd of 10,000.

T

TALLEST PLAYER

It is impossible to say for definite who has been the tallest player ever on Sunderland's books as such records are notoriously unreliable. One of the players certain to lay claim to the title is the club's Republic of Ireland international Niall Quinn who stands at 6ft 4ins.

TAYLOR, ERNIE

Sunderland-born Ernie Taylor was a naval submariner when he joined Newcastle United in 1942. At only 5ft 4ins, Taylor was one of the smallest players in the game, but his defence-splitting passes caused havoc amongst opponents. When Newcastle beat Blackpool in the FA Cup Final of 1951, it was Taylor's cheeky back-heel that laid on a goal for Jackie Milburn. After that defeat, Blackpool's Stanley Matthews told his manager Joe Smith that he would like Taylor in the Seasiders' team.

In October 1951, Taylor joined the Bloomfield Road club for £25,000 and when Matthews had recovered from injury, the pair created one of the most respected right-wing partnerships in the game. In the 1953 FA Cup Final, Taylor played brilliantly in the 4-3 win over Bolton Wanderers and later that year made his one and only appearance for England in the 6-3 defeat by Hungary. He went on to score 55 goals in 242 games for Blackpool before signing for Manchester United in the wake of the Munich disaster.

After making his United debut in the emotional FA Cup match against

Sheffield Wednesday, he helped the Old Trafford side reach Wembley. But Bolton Wanderers ended his dream of picking up a third FA Cup winners' medal with three different clubs.

Before the end of 1958, the skilful and entertaining inside-forward had returned to his home-town club Sunderland in a £6,000 deal.

He made his debut in a 2-0 home defeat by Cardiff City and over the next three seasons scored 11 goals in 71 games before entering non-League football with Altrincham and then crossing the water to play for Derry City.

TEAM OF ALL TALENTS
Sunderland, League Champions in 1891-92, won 13 matches in a row between 14 November 1891 and 2 April 1892 and were known as the 'Team of All Talents' though a better description would be the team of all countries because they only had one English player - their captain, Tom Porteous!

TEST MATCHES
In the early days of the club's history it was customary for the bottom two clubs of the First Division and the top two of the Second Division to play 'Test Matches' to decide which two should be numbered among the 16 clubs of the First Division. There was no automatic promotion and relegation as we know it today.

In 1896-97 Sunderland had finished the season in 15th place in the First Division with Burnley rooted to the foot of the table. The other two teams involved were Notts County and Newton Heath from the Second Division. After losing 1-0 at Notts County, the Wearsiders drew their return home match 0-0 and then drew 1-1 at Newton Heath with Morgan getting the all-important goal. This meant that Sunderland had to win their home match against Newton Heath, which they did 2-0 with both goals being scored by Gillespie, and so preserved their First Division status.

THIRD DIVISION
Sunderland were relegated to the Third Division for the only time in their history after defeat in the two leg play-off against Gillingham at the end of the 1986-87 season.

The club's first game in the Third Division saw a Keith Bertschin goal produce a 1-0 victory at Brentford and two wins and four draws followed before the Wearsiders lost 3-1 at Brighton. New Manager Denis Smith returned to his former club York City and signed Marco Gabbiadini for £80,000. The Nottingham-born forward immediately formed a prolific partnership with Eric Gates which produced 40 goals. Gabbiadini was top scorer with 21 goals whilst Gates' total of 19 included four goals in a 7-0 home win over Southend United and all three in a 3-0 defeat of Rotherham United.

The club for whom new signing John Kay from Wimbledon was ever-present clinched promotion with a 1-0 win at Port Vale on 30 April and then won the Championship following victories over Northampton Town (3-1) and Rotherham United (4-1).

Denis Smith's forecast of an immediate return to the Second Division came true with Sunderland having spent just one of their 97 playing seasons in the Football League in the Third Division.

THOMSON, CHARLIE

Centre-half Charlie Thomson began his career with Heart of Midlothian and after a number of impressive performances for the Scottish League club, he won the first of 21 full caps for his country when he played against Northern Ireland in 1904. In the summer of 1908 he joined Sunderland when there was a £350 limit on transfer fees. Sunderland had to take a second makeweight player and pay £700 for Thomson. He made his debut in the opening game of the 1908-09 season as the Wearsiders went down 1-0 at Manchester City.

Thomson was an important member of the Sunderland side for the next seven seasons and in 1912-13 missed just one game as the Wearsiders won the League Championship. His only goal that campaign was the only one in the match against Championship rivals Sheffield United and gave the club two precious points. Also that season, Thomson who captained the side led the club to the FA Cup Final against Aston Villa, but the northeast club lost 1-0.

Thomson who could take care of himself in any company, went on to play in 265 League and Cup games before retiring at the end of the First World War.

TODD, COLIN

Colin Todd represented Chester-le-Street Boys before signing for Sunderland in July 1964, turning professional on his 18th birthday. He played his first game for the Wearsiders in a 2-0 defeat at Sheffield United in October 1966. An ever-present in 1967-68, he missed very few games in his five seasons with the club, appearing in 195 League and Cup games before joining Derby County for £180,000, a record fee for a defender, in February 1971.

At the Baseball Ground he won two League Championship medals and played in the European Cup. His second League Championship success in 1974-75 was probably his greatest season in which he rarely made an error. At the end of that campaign he was voted the PFA's Footballer of the Year.

Todd moved to Everton for £330,000 in September 1978, switching to Birmingham City twelve months later in another £300,000 deal. He helped the St Andrew's club gain promotion to the First Division in 1979-80 before rejoining Brian Clough at Nottingham Forest for £70,000. He ended a fine playing career with Oxford United, the Manor Ground club winning the Third Division title in 1983-84. When he retired at the end of the following season, he had played in a total of 747 League and Cup games for his six clubs.

After managing Whitley Bay for a while, he was assistant-manager to Bruce Rioch at Middlesbrough, eventually succeeding him as manager. He later became assistant-manager to Rioch again, this time at Bolton Wanderers where he played an important role in the club's promotion to the Premier League and in the Wanderers' Cup exploits which culminated in them reaching the League Cup Final at Wembley in 1995. When Rioch left, Todd took over the reins and though he couldn't prevent them being relegated, led them back to the Premiership as champions in 1996-97. The Wanderers were relegated again after just one season in the top flight and Todd now in his eighth year with the Lancashire club aims to lead them back to the Premiership for a third time, after reaching the play-off final in 1998-99.

TOURS

Sunderland's first ever tour was in May 1909 when a lengthy trip was made to Budapest, Vienna, Prague, Munich and Nuremburg, taking in eight games. The close season tours abroad were a regular feature of the club's programme and in 1913 the club won all eight games of its tour to Hungary, Austria and Germany, scoring 39 goals and conceding just five. Included in that record was a 9-0 win over Hungarian side Fereneznurisa Tora Club in the opening game of the tour.

In 1969, the Wearsiders toured Germany and Italy and beat Schutterf 10-0, their biggest victory on foreign soil. In 1976 the club toured Tahiti, New Zealand, Singapore and Australia and were undefeated in 10 games with Mel Holden scoring all five goals in a 5-0 win over Tasmania.

TOWERS, TONY

An England Schoolboy international, Tony Towers began his career with his home-town club Manchester City, where he added Youth and Under-23 honours to his name. When City won the European Cup Winners' Cup in 1969-70, Towers was the substitute who scored in extra-time to give the club victory over Academica de Coimbra in the second leg of the quarter-final. He went on to score 12 goals in 159 first team games before being transferred to Sunderland for £100,000 plus Mick Horswill, who made the switch to Maine Road.

Towers made his Sunderland debut in a 1-0 home win over Fulham in March 1974 and played in eight games, scoring in each of the last two games of the season. He missed just one game in 1974-75 and the following season was a big influence in the club's midfield as they won the Second Division championship. Towers scored 10 goals in 34 league games including the all-important winner against Bolton Wanderers in

Tony Towers

the penultimate home game of the season - whenever Towers scored, the Wearsiders did not lose!

His form led to him winning three full caps for England whilst with the north-east club, his first against Wales in May 1976. At the end of the club's first season back in Division One, Towers, who had scored 22 goals in 121 games left Roker Park to join Birmingham City for a fee of £140,000.

Sadly, he was a huge disappointment at St Andrew's, where his better performances came at the tail end of his spell with the club when he was acting as a sweeper. He later played for Montreal Manic, Tampa Bay Rowdies and Vancouver Whitecaps before turning out as a non-contract player with Rochdale.

TRANSFERS
The club's record transfer fee received is £1.5 million from Crystal Palace for Marco Gabbiadini in September 1991.

The club's record transfer fee paid is £2.5 million to rivals Newcastle United for midfielder Lee Clark in June 1997.

TUEART, DENIS
A former Newcastle Boys player, Denis Tueart slipped through the St James' Park net when Sunderland signed him from Wellbech Juniors in 1966.

After making his debut in a goalless home draw against Sheffield Wednesday on Boxing Day 1968 he became a regular in the Sunderland side. The highlight of Tueart's Sunderland career was undoubtedly the Wearsider's victory over Leeds United in the FA Cup Final of 1973. Tueart who scored his only hat-trick for the club in a 4-1 home win over Swindon Town in 1973-74, also scored in both legs of the European Cup Winners' Cup first round tie against Vasas Budapest, both of which were won by the north-east club.

After Sunderland's exit from the competition in the second round at the hands of Sporting Lisbon, Denis Tueart, who had scored 56 goals in 222 games, left Roker Park in March 1974 to join Manchester City for a fee of £275,000, then a record fee for both clubs.

Within days of his arrival at Maine Road, he had received international recognition when he was selected to play for the Football League against the Scottish League, and scored in a 5-0 win. In December 1974 he was selected as an over-age player in England's Under-23 side against Scotland at Pittodrie and scored twice in his only appearance at that level in a 3-0 win. In May 1975 at the end of his first full season with City, he won the first of six full caps when he played against Cyprus in Limassol.

In 1975-76 he was the club's top scorer with 24 League and Cup goals and clinched victory in the League Cup final with a spectacular overhead kick. His best league season as a goalscorer with the Maine Road club was 1976-77 when he netted 18 goals in 38 games as City finished runners-up to Liverpool in the First Division.

In February 1978 he joined New York Cosmos for £250,000 but returned to Maine Road early in 1980 for £150,000 and collected an FA Cup runners-up medal with the club in 1981. After scoring 107 goals in 267 games he left Maine Road for a second time and joined Stoke City on a free transfer. He ended his league career with Burnley before briefly appearing with Irish League club, Derry City.

Dennis Tueart

TURNER, CHRIS

Goalkeeper Chris Turner began his Football League career with Sheffield Wednesday and made his debut for the Owls in a goalless draw at home to Walsall on the opening day of the 1976-77 season. In fact, that season, the young 'keeper was in such good form that he played in five games for the England Youth team. Turner kept 15 clean sheets in his first season including four in succession but in the summer of 1979 he was allowed to leave

Hillsborough and joined Sunderland for £90,000.

After making his debut in a 1-1 home draw against Preston North End on 29 September 1979, he played in 30 games that season, keeping 13 clean sheets as the club won promotion to the First Division. For the next three seasons he shared the goalkeeping duties with Barry Siddall but was ever-present in seasons 1983-84 and 1984-85. He had played in 224 League and Cup games for the Wearsiders when he signed for Manchester United for what was then a club record fee for a goalkeeper of £250,000.

Despite competition from Gary Bailey, he played in 79 games, but left the club in 1988 to return to Sheffield Wednesday. He took his tally of league games for the club to 166 before seeing out his career with Leyton Orient after a loan spell at Leeds United.

Chris Turner

U

UNDEFEATED

Sunderland have remained undefeated at home throughout six league seasons: 1891-92; 1892-93; 1894-95; 1895-96; 1975-76; and 1979-80. The club's best and longest undefeated home sequence in the Football League is 44 matches between 18 October 1890 and 6 December 1893. Sunderland's longest run of undefeated league matches home and away is 16 between 11 November 1922 and 24 February 1923.

UTILITY PLAYERS

A utility player is one of those particularly gifted footballers who can play in several, or even many, different positions. One of Sunderland's earliest utility players was Harry Low. Signed from Aberdeen, Low was an unusually versatile player, who was equally at home at full-back, half-back, centre-half, inside-forward or centre-forward!

After the mid 1960s, players were encouraged to become more adaptable and to see their roles as less stereotyped. At the same time however, much less attention was paid to the implication of wearing a certain numbered shirt and accordingly some of the more versatile players came to wear almost all the different numbered shirts at some stage or another, although this did not necessarily indicate a vast variety of positions. In the modern game, Gordon Armstrong, Kevin Ball, John Kay and Gary Rowell among others have worn a variety of outfield shirts.

V

VENISON, BARRY

Barry Venison first came to Sunderland as a 14-year-old associated schoolboy before signing as an apprentice after leaving school. He made his Football League debut in a 2-0 defeat at Notts County in October 1981, just a couple of months after his 17th birthday. By the time he turned professional he had appeared in a further nine league games. His first two seasons with the Wearsiders saw him alternate between right-back and midfield but after that he became firmly established at right-back, missing only four league games in two years. Also at this time, Venison was a regular member of the England Under-21 team and won 10 caps at this level.

He became the youngest Wembley Cup Final captain when at the age of 20, he led Sunderland to the 1985 League Cup Final against Norwich City. At the end of that 1984-85 season, the club were relegated to the Second Division and after one season in Division Two in which he was again switched between full-back and midfield, he left to join Liverpool for £200,000.

The Anfield club were the only ones to take up his round robin letter to First Division clubs offering his services. Venison had played in 207 games for the Wearsiders and arrived on Merseyside as a replacement for Phil Neal. In six seasons with Liverpool he never truly established himself as a first team regular, tending to only be selected when Steve Nicol was required for other duties. Nevertheless he shared in the Liverpool success story, winning League Championship medals in 1987-88 and 1989-90, plus winning an FA Cup winners' medal in 1989. After being struck down by injury, he lost his place to Rob Jones and after failing to win a place in Liverpool's Cup Final squad against Sunderland in 1992, it came as no surprise when he returned to the north-east to join Newcastle United.

At the end of his first season on Tyneside, he had helped the Magpies win promotion to the Premier League as First Division Champions.

Capped twice at full international level whilst with United, he went on to appear in 133 games before joining Turkish side Galatasaray, who were managed by his former boss at Anfield, Graeme Souness. In October 1995 he returned to the Premier League with Southampton and gave the Saints' young side valuable experience. Appointed captain, a continuing back problem limited his appearances and eventually forced his retirement from the game.

Barry Venison

VICTORIES IN A SEASON - HIGHEST
In the 1998-99 season, Sunderland won 31 of their 46 league fixtures to win the First Division Championship, the highest number of wins in the club's history.

VICTORIES IN A SEASON - LOWEST
Sunderland's poorest performance was in 1969-70 when they won only six matches out of their 42 league games and finished 21st in the First Division.

VICTORY LEAGUE
Sunderland were one of eight clubs that participated in a competition known as 'The Victory League' in 1919. The club's record was as follows:

P	W	D	L	F	A	Pts
14	8	2	4	31	20	18

A number of 'guest' players, the most famous being Jimmy Seed represented the club in a season in which the club's biggest win was 6-1 at home to Scotswood and Jackie Mordue scored a hat-trick in a 4-3 defeat at Newcastle United.

Dave Watson

WARTIME FOOTBALL

Despite the outbreak of war in 1914, the major football leagues embarked upon their planned programme of matches for the ensuing season and these were completed on schedule at the end of April the following year. Sunderland finished eighth in Division One, scoring 81 goals including a 6-0 win at Tottenham Hotspur.

After four years of hostilities, football recommenced in the north-east with the Victory League, a competition in which 'guest' players were allowed.

In contrast to the events of 1914, once war was declared on 3 September 1939, the football league programme of 1939-40 was immediately suspended and the government forbade any major sporting events so that for a short while there was no football of any description. Sunderland had opened the season with a 3-0 victory over Derby County but followed that with two defeats against Huddersfield Town (1-2) and Arsenal (2-5).

It was 1941-42 before Sunderland embarked on any competitive football during the war years, playing in the North League and the League War Cup. In this latter competition, Cliff Whitelum scored four goals on two occasions as Middlesbrough were beaten 6-0 and York City 8-3. The following season the club also participated in and won the West Riding FA Cup, beating Huddersfield Town 7-6 on aggregate in the final. In the first leg of that tie, Cliff Whitelum scored all the club's six goals in a 6-2 home win. Whitelum started the following North League campaign in sparkling form with seven goals in the opening two matches against Leeds United, netting four in a 7-1 home win and a hat-trick in a 5-1 triumph at Elland Road.

In 1944-45 Sunderland reached the final of the Tyne-Tees-Wear Cup but lost 6-3 against Gateshead.

WATSON, DAVE

Dave Watson played for Stapleford Old Boys before joining Notts County and was a centre-forward first and foremost. He moved on to Rotherham United where he was switched to centre-half by Millmoor boss Tommy Docherty. In December 1970 he joined Sunderland for a fee of £100,000 and scored on his debut in a 1-1 draw at Watford as he reverted back to his centre-forward role. In 1971-72 he scored 15 League and Cup goals but his career really took off the following season when he moved to centre-half. He won an FA Cup winners' medal in 1973 and after three seasons of outstanding performances, Watson won the first of 65 England caps (14 won whilst with Sunderland) when he played against Portugal in 1974.

In the summer of 1975, Watson who had scored 33 goals in 209 League and Cup games left Roker Park to join Manchester City for £275,000.

At Maine Road he won a League Cup winners' medal and made 185 appearances before going overseas to play for Werder Bremen. He returned to these shores in October 1979 when he signed for Southampton for £200,000. After two and a half seasons at The Dell he joined Stoke City for £50,000. It turned out to be a good investment as Stoke enjoyed one and a half good seasons at the end of Watson's career.

He was released to go on an 'illegal' tour to South Africa which eventually failed to materialise, but finally moved to play for Vancouver Whitecaps in the NASL. On his return he linked up with Derby County, later playing for Fort Lauderdale Sun, Notts County (Again) and Kettering Town.

WATSON, JIMMY

Jimmy Watson began his football career with Burnbank, a Lanarkshire junior side. After he turned down an offer from Hearts, he signed for Clyde and his displays at full-back quickly brought him to the attention of Sunderland who secured his services in January 1900.

Watson made his debut for the Wearsiders in a goalless home draw against Glossop North End a month after joining the club. He was to spend eight successful seasons at Roker Park, appearing in 225 League and Cup games and winning a League Championship medal in 1901-02.

The tough-tackling full-back also won four full caps for Scotland with three of his appearances being against England.

In April 1907 he joined Middlesbrough and in 1907-08 was ever-present. In 1909 he won two further caps and the following year was appointed 'Boro's assistant-trainer for a spell before ending his career with Shildon. He later emigrated to Canada and in the 1920s was coaching in that country.

WATSON, TOM

One of the game's first great managers, Tom Watson was appointed Sunderland's match secretary and manager before the start of the 1889-90 season. At Sunderland he produced the 'Team of All Talents' which won the League Championship three times, taking the title in 1891-92, 1892-93 and 1894-95. In the club's first season in the Football League, Watson took them to the semi-final of the FA Cup where they lost to Notts County after a replay. The Reds also reached the semi-final stage in 1892 when they lost 4-1 to Aston Villa and then went down to the Midlands side again at the same stage three years later, 2-1.

In 1891-92 the club won all 13 of their home games and the following season scored 100 goals in their 30 games. In 1893-94 Sunderland were runners-up to Aston Villa before winning the title for a third time in the space of four seasons.

Despite running his own tobacconist shop in Monkwearmouth Station since 1894, Watson accepted a higher pay offer from Liverpool to become their manager. Though he took a little time to build the Anfield club up to be a force to be reckoned with, he did lead them to the League Championship for the first time in 1900-01. Though they were relegated to the Second Division in 1903-04 they returned to the top flight as champions the following season. The following year they became the first club to take the Second and First Division titles in consecutive seasons. Watson also took the club to the FA Cup Final in 1914 but despite dominating most of the match, they lost 1-0 to Burnley.

A great character and very popular with all the players who served under him, he was still in office when he died in May 1915.

Sunderland's full league record under Tom Watson is:

P	W	D	L	F	A
168	106	25	37	448	225

WATSON, WILLIE

One of the few people to be capped by England at both football and cricket, Willie Watson began his career with Huddersfield Town, making 11 league appearances before the outbreak of the Second World War.

He signed for Sunderland in April 1946 for a fee of £8,000 and made his debut in a 3-2 home win over Derby County on the opening day of the 1946-47 season. Never a prolific goalscorer, his five goals in that campaign being his best return. He missed very few games over the next seven seasons, playing in 223 League and Cup matches for the Wearsiders before leaving to become player-manager of Halifax Town.

In November 1949 he made his debut for England in a 9-2 win over Northern Ireland at Maine Road, the first of four caps. Watson also played in 22 Tests for England, having joined Yorkshire in 1939 and being awarded his county cap in 1947.

Watson had two spells in charge of Halifax Town but did not achieve much success. However, he did produce a number of good players, but the Yorkshire club were always in financial difficulties and were forced to sell their better players. He also managed Bradford City where he laid the foundations for a future promotion side.

Watson's cricketing career was of a much higher profile and after leaving Yorkshire, he captained Leicestershire. He was also an England cricket selector and was player-manager of the MCC tour party to East Africa in 1963.

WEATHER CONDITIONS

On Saturday 1 September 1906, Sunderland visited St James' Park for the opening game of the 1906-07 season. A crowd of 56,375, a new record, watched the Magpies win 4-2 after a terrific game played in sweltering heat. The temperature on the St James' pitch was 91F - the hottest day recorded in British football. The United players wore white sun caps with the peaks reversed as protection against sunstroke, while Jimmy Watson, the Sunderland left-back collapsed from the heat.

WEST, COLIN

Born in Wallsend, Colin West was a burly striker who made his Sunderland debut as a substitute in a 2-1 defeat at West Bromwich Albion in April 1981. He started his first match the following November as the Wearsiders crashed 5-1 at home to Manchester United. Over the next two seasons he was in and out of the side before winning a regular place in 1983-84.

Particularly good in the air and possessing a fierce long-range shot, West went on to score 29 goals in 129 first team appearances for Sunderland before leaving Roker Park to join Watford in March 1985 for a fee of £115,000. In a little over a year, West's 23 goals in 56 games for the Vicarage Road club led to him moving to Glasgow Rangers for £180,000 in the summer of 1986. The majority of his 15 appearances for the Ibrox club were as a substitute and it came as no surprise when he returned to the Football League with Sheffield Wednesday in September 1987.

After scoring 13 goals in 60 games for the Owls, he was on the move again, this time to West Bromwich Albion where his experience helped the Baggies in their fight against relegation to the Third Division. After a loan spell at Port Vale he joined Swansea City on a free transfer before signing for Leyton Orient in the summer of 1993. He was the club's top scorer in his first three seasons at Brisbane Road but after a loan spell at Northampton Town, the much-travelled striker left to join Rushden and Diamonds.

WILSON, HUGH
Hugh Wilson was born at Mauchline, Ayrshire in 1869 and first played for the Newmilns club. He joined Sunderland in 1890 and made his debut in the club's first-ever game in the Football League when they lost 3-2 at home to Burnley. He remained with the Wearsiders for nine years, playing mainly as a half-back before later moving to play in the forward line. Wilson scored some important goals and netted a hat-trick in a 3-0 home win over Bury in October 1898. Indeed, he could fill in at full-back and even played as a goalkeeper in an emergency. He captained Sunderland and his long throw-ins were a great feature of his game. He had scored 45 goals in 258 first team games when he left the club in May 1899 to join Bedminster.

He was captain of Bedminster for the 1899-1900 season and stayed when they amalgamated with Bristol City to play for a further season with the 'new' club.

He later returned to Scotland to play for Third Lanark where he won his fourth full cap for Scotland. One contemporary writer said of him 'He is never content with doing one man's work on the field - if ever a man gave all he possessed in the way of his natural talents to his employers, that man was Hugh Wilson'.

WORST START
The club's worst-ever start to a season was in 1969-70. It took 11 league games to record their first victory, drawing three and losing seven of the opening fixtures. The run ended with a 2-1 home win over Nottingham Forest on 20

September 1969. At the end of the season in which the club only won six games they were, not surprisingly relegated to the Second Division.

The club also failed to win until the 11th game of the 1976-77 season when once again they lost their First Division status. They drew four and lost six of their first ten matches before beating Coventry City 2-1 at Highfield Road on 30 October 1976.

WRIGHT, ARTHUR

An England Schoolboy international, wing-half Arthur Wright joined the club straight from Castletown School in September 1936 and made his debut as an 18-year-old in April 1938 in a goalless home draw against Leeds United. He played 12 games at the beginning of the 1938-39 season before losing his place to Alex Hastings and appeared in a number of wartime games.

After the hostilities, Wright missed very few games over the next eight seasons and was ever-present in 1948-49 as the club finished eighth in Division One. Never a prolific scorer, netting 14 goals in 283 League and Cup games, his first for the club was the winner in the 2-1 defeat of Blackburn Rovers in February 1947, followed by another decisive strike in the 2-1 home win over Sheffield United the following month.

He played his last game for the club against Sheffield United at Bramall Lane in March 1955 after which he hung up his boots and became the club's trainer-coach.

WRIGHT, TOMMY

Tommy Wright joined Sunderland from Partick Thistle for a fee of £9,000 in March 1949 and made his debut in a 4-1 defeat at Portsmouth. The following season when Sunderland finished third in Division One, Wright was an ever-present and scored 13 goals including his only hat-trick for the club in a 4-2 home win over Everton. He reached double figures again the following season before being hampered by injuries in 1951-52. He was back to his best in 1952-53 and at the end of the season won three full caps for Scotland. His best season in terms of goals scored was 1953-54 when he netted 18 in 38 games, but in January 1955 after he had scored 55 goals in 180 League and Cup outings, he returned north of the border when he joined East Fife in the deal that brought Charlie Fleming to Roker Park.

Two years later, he returned to the Football League with Oldham Athletic but hung up his boots after just one season with the Boundary Park club. His son Tommy played for Leeds United, Oldham Athletic and Leicester City.

X

'X'

In football 'x' traditionally stands for a draw. The club record for the number of draws in a season was in 1954-55 and 1994-95 when they drew 18 of their matches.

XMAS DAY

There was a time when Football League matches were regularly played on Christmas Day but in recent years the game's authorities have dropped the fixture from their calendar. The last time Sunderland played on Christmas Day was 1956 when a Billy Bingham goal was enough to beat Aston Villa in front of a Roker Park crowd of 18,543. The first occasion that Sunderland played a league game on Christmas Day was 1891 when they beat Everton 4-0 at Anfield. Of the 13 league games the club played on Christmas Day up until the outbreak of the First World War, their best win was 5-2 over Newcastle United in 1914 when Robert Best scored a hat-trick. Sunderland only lost two of those fixtures but in the years between the wars, the club only won one of their ten matches and that was in 1937 when they beat Huddersfield Town 2-1. During that period the club lost a number of high-scoring games - Bolton Wanderers (2-6) Everton (4-5 and 2-6) Blackburn Rovers (3-5) and Leicester City (2-5). After the Second World War, Sunderland regained some of their earlier Christmas Day form, though in 1951 they went down 4-1 at home to Newcastle United in front of a Roker Park crowd of 52,274.

Y

YOUNGEST PLAYER
The youngest player to appear in a first-class fixture for Sunderland is goal-keeper Derek Forster who played in the First Division match against Leicester City (Home 3-3) on 22 August 1964 when he was 15 years 184 days old.

YOUTH CUP
Sunderland have appeared in the FA Youth Cup Final on three occasions. Their aggregate scores were:

1966	Arsenal 5	Sunderland 3
1967	Sunderland 2	Birmingham City 0
1969	Sunderland 6	West Bromwich Albion 3

Z

ZENITH
The 1912-13 season was the most successful in the club's history as they came very close to winning the elusive League and FA Cup double.

After a creditable draw at Newcastle United on the opening day of the season, the Wearsiders lost four on the trot and it was not until their eighth game of the season, that they registered their first win when they beat Middlesbrough 4-0 at Roker Park. It was the worst start ever made by a Championship-winning side but from mid October the club never looked back. Having lost five matches in the previous two months, they only lost another four over the next six months in the league. Such was the gap that they had to make up however, that it was not until two-thirds of the 38 fixtures had been played, that the Wearsiders appeared in the top three. By November, the club got into their stride and beat Liverpool 7-0 with Charlie Buchan scoring five of the goals. Holley netted a hat-trick in a 5-1 win at Bradford City before Sunderland beat their rivals Aston Villa 3-1 at the end of the month.

In the FA Cup, Sunderland took nine matches to reach the final. In round one, four goals by Jimmy Richardson helped them beat Clapton Orient 6-0 but after that, progress was much harder. Manchester City were beaten 2-0 at Roker Park after the first game at Hyde Road had been abandoned and non-League Swindon Town were defeated 4-2 to set up a quarter-final meeting with Newcastle United. The tie went to three matches before two goals from Jackie Mordue helped Sunderland win 3-0. In the semi-final, Sunderland and Burnley played out a goalless draw before goals from Buchan, Mordue and Holley gave the Wearsiders a 3-2 win after they had trailed 2-1. In the final, Sunderland met arch rivals Aston Villa but Tom Barber scored the only goal of a highly charged and controversial match to take the Cup to the Midlands.

On the Wednesday after the final, the two teams had to meet in the league at Villa Park. Both sides were forced to make changes and Sunderland for whom Tinsley opened the scoring were glad to come away with a point in a 1-1 draw. With only two games remaining, Sunderland needed just one point to make certain of the title, which they got the following Saturday in a 3-1 win against Bolton Wanderers at Burnden Park. They then won their final match against Bradford City 1-0 to end the season as League Champions, four points clear of Aston Villa.

ZENITH DATA SYSTEMS CUP

The Zenith Data Systems Cup replaced the Simod Cup in the 1989-90 season. Sunderland's first match in the competition saw them go out at the first hurdle, losing 2-1 at Port Vale. In 1990-91 the Wearsiders drew 2-2 at Notts County before beating their Meadow Lane opponents 3-1 in a penalty shoot out. In the quarter-final, Sunderland travelled to Goodison Park to play Everton but were beaten 4-1 with all the home side's goals being scored by Tony Cottee.